Large Language Models (LLMs)

Maria Johnsen

Preface

This book offers an in-depth exploration of the world of Artificial Intelligence (AI) and Natural Language Processing (NLP), with a special focus on Large Language Models (LLMs). It is designed with academics in mind, making it a perfect resource for students and researchers.

Starting with a foundational introduction to AI and its subfields, the book traces the evolution of NLP from rule-based systems to advanced neural networks. It explains the core concepts and architecture of neural networks, highlighting the transformative impact of transformers and attention mechanisms—crucial components for understanding how LLMs process natural language. Detailed explanations of encoder-decoder structures, positional encoding, and various types of neural networks provide a solid technical grounding.

A significant portion of the book is dedicated to the practical aspects of working with LLMs. It covers data collection and preprocessing techniques, training objectives, optimization algorithms, and methods for scaling up models. The transition from GPT-2 to GPT-4 is used as a case study to illustrate the computational challenges and advancements in the field.

The applications of LLMs are explored across various industries, showcasing their impact on customer service, content creation, journalism, healthcare, and education. Additionally, the book delves into the integration of text with other modalities in multimodal models and the capabilities of zero-shot and few-shot learning.

Ethical considerations are a key focus, with discussions on understanding and mitigating bias in LLMs, ensuring responsible AI use, and addressing regulatory and legal implications. The future of LLMs is also contemplated, with predictions for emerging trends and technologies.

To provide practical guidance, the book includes chapters on setting up the environment, building and optimizing simple language models, and deploying LLMs in production. It concludes with recommendations for further reading and resources, encouraging continuous learning in this rapidly evolving field.

"Large Language Models (LLM)" is a comprehensive resource for anyone interested in understanding, developing, and applying LLMs, from beginners to advanced practitioners. Students are encouraged to buy this book to deepen their knowledge and enhance their academic pursuits.

Table of Contents

Summary

Explore the fascinating world of Large Language Models (LLMs) with this comprehensive and accessible guide. Whether you're just starting out or have years of experience in artificial intelligence and natural language processing, this book has something for everyone.

Embark on a journey through the evolution of language models, from their humble beginnings to today's groundbreaking advancements. Discover how neural networks and transformers have revolutionized language processing and generation. Learn all about training LLMs, from gathering and preparing data to fine-tuning models for specific tasks.

Understand the real-world applications of LLMs across

various industries, including customer service, content creation, healthcare, and education. See how these powerful tools are making a difference and transforming our interaction with technology.

Get hands-on with practical techniques for generating text, maintaining context, and controlling output quality. Dive into advanced topics like multimodal models, zero-shot learning, and multilingual text processing to stay ahead in this rapidly evolving field.

This book also addresses the ethical aspects of using LLMs, offering guidance on mitigating bias and ensuring responsible use. With insights into the future of LLMs, you'll be well-prepared for the next wave of innovations.

Written in an engaging and approachable style, this guide makes complex concepts easy to understand and apply. Whether you're a student, researcher, or professional, you'll find valuable knowledge and practical advice to enhance your understanding and use of large language models.

Chapter 1 AI and Natural Language Processing

Artificial Intelligence (AI) refers to the simulation of human intelligence in machines that are programmed to think and act like humans. This field encompasses a broad range of technologies and techniques, enabling machines to perform tasks that typically require human intelligence. AI aims to improve efficiency, accuracy, and decision-making capabilities across various domains. The overarching goal is to create systems capable of performing complex tasks, adapting to new situations, and improving through experience.

AI is divided into several subfields, each focusing on different aspects of intelligent behavior and problem-solving. These subfields include:

Machine Learning (ML)

Machine Learning (ML) is a pivotal subset of Artificial Intelligence (AI) focused on developing algorithms that empower computers to learn from data and make informed decisions. By harnessing the power of data, ML systems can identify patterns, make predictions, and improve over time without explicit programming for each task. This transformative technology encompasses several key techniques and has evolved into more specialized areas such as deep learning, which further pushes the boundaries of what machines can achieve.

Key Techniques in Machine Learning

Machine learning employs various techniques to process data and extract meaningful insights. Among these techniques, supervised learning, unsupervised learning, and reinforcement learning are the most prominent.

Supervised Learning

Supervised learning is a technique where the model is trained using labeled data. This means that each training example includes an input-output pair, with the output serving as the correct answer. The goal is for the model to learn the mapping from inputs to outputs so that it can accurately predict the output for new, unseen inputs.

- Applications: Supervised learning is widely used in applications such as spam detection, where emails are classified as spam or not spam; image classification, where images are labeled with the objects they contain; and predictive analytics, where future trends are forecasted based on historical data.

Unsupervised Learning

In unsupervised learning, the data provided to the model is

unlabeled. The model's task is to identify patterns and structures within the data without any prior knowledge of the outcomes. This technique is particularly useful for exploring data and finding hidden insights.

- Applications: Common applications of unsupervised learning include clustering, where data points are grouped into clusters based on similarity (e.g., customer segmentation); anomaly detection, where unusual data points are identified (e.g., fraud detection); and association rule learning, which finds interesting relationships between variables (e.g., market basket analysis).

Reinforcement Learning

Reinforcement learning involves training a model to make sequences of decisions by rewarding desired behaviors and punishing undesired ones. The model learns by interacting with an environment, aiming to maximize cumulative rewards over time.

- Applications: Reinforcement learning is prominently used in robotics for autonomous control, gaming AI (such as AlphaGo, which defeated human champions in the game of Go), and adaptive systems like personalized recommendations and dynamic pricing strategies.

Deep Learning: A Specialized Subset of Machine Learning

Deep learning, a subset of machine learning, leverages neural networks with multiple layers—hence the term "deep"—to analyze and interpret complex data. This approach mimics the human brain's structure and function, enabling machines to process data in intricate ways.

Definition and Mechanism

Deep learning utilizes artificial neural networks that consist of layers of nodes (neurons). Each layer transforms the input data in a nonlinear way, allowing the network to learn hierarchical representations of the data. The depth of the network refers to the number of layers it has, with deeper networks capable of capturing more abstract and complex features.

Applications of Deep Learning

Deep learning has revolutionized various fields by achieving remarkable performance in tasks that were previously challenging for traditional machine learning models. Some of its notable applications include:

- Image and Speech Recognition: Deep learning models, such as convolutional neural networks (CNNs), have set new benchmarks in image classification and object detection. Similarly, recurrent neural networks (RNNs) and transformers have excelled in speech recognition and synthesis, leading to advancements in voice-activated assistants like Siri and Alexa.

- Natural Language Processing (NLP): Deep learning techniques have significantly improved NLP tasks such as machine translation, sentiment analysis, and text generation. Models like BERT and GPT have enabled machines to understand and generate human language with high accuracy, enhancing applications like chatbots and automated content creation.

- Autonomous Systems: Deep learning is at the core of developing autonomous systems, including self-driving cars and drones. These systems rely on deep neural networks to perceive their environment, make real-time decisions, and navigate safely, demonstrating the potential of deep learning in transforming industries.

Machine learning, with its diverse techniques of supervised, unsupervised, and reinforcement learning, forms the backbone of modern AI applications. Deep learning, a powerful subset of ML, has further expanded the horizons of what machines can achieve, particularly in complex tasks such as image and speech recognition, natural language processing, and autonomous systems. As data continues to grow exponentially, the capabilities of machine learning and deep learning will only continue to evolve, driving innovation and transforming the way we interact with technology.

Natural Language Processing (NLP)

Natural Language Processing (NLP) is a crucial subfield of artificial intelligence (AI) that focuses on the interaction between computers and human language. It encompasses the development of algorithms and systems that enable computers to understand, interpret, and generate human language in a way that is both meaningful and useful. The primary goal of NLP is to bridge the gap between human communication and computer understanding, allowing machines to process and respond to text or speech in natural language in a way that is similar to how humans do.

Key Components of NLP

- Understanding: This involves the ability of a computer to process input text or speech and comprehend its meaning. Understanding natural language requires a deep knowledge of grammar, syntax, semantics, and context. For example, understanding the difference between homonyms based on context (like "bank" as a financial institution versus "bank" as the side of a river) is a fundamental aspect of NLP.

- Interpretation: Interpretation goes beyond mere

understanding to deduce the intent behind the words. It involves analyzing the nuances and implied meanings within a text or conversation. This is particularly important in tasks such as sentiment analysis where the objective is to gauge the emotional tone behind a series of words.

- Generation: This aspect of NLP focuses on creating human-like text or speech. It involves generating responses, summaries, translations, or new content based on the input received. The goal is to produce language that is coherent, contextually appropriate, and syntactically correct.

Applications of NLP

The advancements in NLP have led to its widespread adoption across various domains, enhancing the capabilities of numerous applications. Here are some prominent

applications of NLP:

Language Translation

Language translation is one of the most well-known

applications of NLP. Machine translation systems, such as

Google Translate, have significantly improved over the years,

thanks to NLP techniques. These systems are capable of

translating text from one language to another while

preserving the meaning and context of the original text.

Key Techniques in Language Translation:

- Statistical Machine Translation (SMT): Early machine

translation systems relied on statistical models that analyzed

the probabilities of word sequences. While effective to some

extent, SMT struggled with maintaining context and fluency.

- Neural Machine Translation (NMT): Modern translation

systems leverage deep learning techniques, specifically neural networks, to improve translation accuracy. NMT systems use large datasets to train models that understand and generate translations with greater fluency and contextual relevance.

Impact of Language Translation

Language translation systems have made significant contributions to global communication, enabling people to access information and communicate across language barriers. They are widely used in international business, travel, education, and even personal interactions on social media platforms.

Sentiment Analysis

Sentiment analysis, also known as opinion mining, is an application of NLP that focuses on determining the emotional tone behind a series of words. It involves analyzing texts to classify them as positive, negative, or neutral. Sentiment analysis is extensively used in various industries to gauge public opinion, customer satisfaction, and market trends.

Key Techniques in Sentiment Analysis

- Lexicon-Based Methods: These methods use predefined lists of words associated with positive or negative sentiments. The sentiment of a text is determined based on the occurrence and frequency of these words.

- Machine Learning-Based Methods: Modern sentiment analysis systems utilize machine learning algorithms to train models on labeled datasets. These models can learn to identify sentiments based on contextual cues and patterns within the text.

Impact of Sentiment Analysis

Sentiment analysis has become an invaluable tool for businesses and organizations. It enables them to monitor customer feedback, brand reputation, and market sentiment in real-time. For instance, companies can use sentiment analysis to analyze reviews and social media posts to improve their products and services. Additionally, sentiment analysis is used in finance to predict stock market trends based on news sentiment.

Chatbots

Chatbots are interactive agents that use NLP to engage in conversations with users. They can be found in customer service, virtual assistants, and various other applications where automated, real-time interaction with users is required. Chatbots are designed to understand user queries and provide relevant responses, simulating a human-like conversation.

Key Techniques in Chatbots:

- Rule-Based Chatbots: These chatbots follow predefined rules and patterns to generate responses. While simple to implement, they are limited in their ability to handle complex or unexpected queries.

- AI-Powered Chatbots: Modern chatbots leverage machine learning and NLP to understand and respond to user inputs more flexibly. They use techniques such as natural language understanding (NLU) and natural language generation (NLG) to process queries and generate appropriate responses.

Impact of Chatbots

Chatbots have revolutionized customer service by providing instant and efficient responses to customer inquiries. They are widely used in e-commerce, banking, healthcare, and various other sectors to handle routine tasks, freeing up human agents to focus on more complex issues. Additionally, virtual assistants like Amazon's Alexa and Apple's Siri are examples of sophisticated chatbots that use NLP to perform a wide range of tasks, from setting reminders to controlling smart home devices.

Information Retrieval

Information retrieval involves extracting relevant information from large datasets, documents, or the web. NLP plays a crucial role in improving the accuracy and efficiency of information retrieval systems, making it easier for users to find the information they need.

Key Techniques in Information Retrieval

- Keyword-Based Search: Traditional search engines rely on keyword matching to retrieve relevant documents. While effective, this approach often returns results that are not contextually relevant.

- Semantic Search: Modern information retrieval systems use NLP to understand the meaning behind queries and documents. They leverage techniques such as entity recognition, relationship extraction, and semantic analysis to provide more accurate and contextually relevant results.

Impact of Information Retrieval

Improved information retrieval systems have enhanced the way people search for information. They are widely used in search engines, digital libraries, and enterprise systems to provide users with quick access to relevant data. For example, search engines like Google use advanced NLP techniques to understand user queries and deliver precise results, improving the overall search experience.

Text Summarization

Text summarization involves condensing a large body of text into a shorter version while preserving its key information and meaning. NLP techniques are used to automate the summarization process, making it easier to digest large volumes of information quickly.

Key Techniques in Text Summarization:

- Extractive Summarization: This approach involves selecting and extracting the most important sentences or phrases from the original text to create a summary. It relies on identifying key sentences based on factors such as frequency, relevance, and position.

- Abstractive Summarization: Abstractive summarization generates new sentences that convey the main ideas of the original text. It involves understanding the context and semantics of the text and then generating concise summaries that may not use the exact words from the original text.

Impact of Text Summarization

Automated text summarization has numerous applications in various fields. It is used in news aggregation to provide quick summaries of news articles, in academic research to summarize papers, and in business to condense reports and documents. This helps users save time and focus on the most important information.

Named Entity Recognition (NER)

Named Entity Recognition (NER) is an NLP technique that identifies and classifies named entities in a text into predefined categories such as names of people, organizations, locations, dates, and more. NER is a fundamental component of many NLP applications.

Key Techniques in NER:

- Rule-Based Methods: These methods use predefined patterns and rules to identify named entities. While simple, they may not generalize well to different domains or languages.

- Machine Learning-Based Methods: Modern NER systems use machine learning algorithms to train models on annotated datasets. These models can recognize named entities based on contextual cues and patterns in the text.

Impact of NER:

NER is widely used in information extraction, search engines, and data analysis. For instance, it helps search engines identify and categorize different types of information within web pages, improving search accuracy. In data analysis, NER is used to extract and organize information from large datasets, making it easier to analyze and interpret the data.

Speech Recognition

Speech recognition, also known as automatic speech recognition (ASR), involves converting spoken language into written text. NLP techniques are used to enhance the accuracy of speech recognition systems, enabling them to understand and transcribe spoken words more effectively.

Key Techniques in Speech Recognition:

- Acoustic Modeling: This involves modeling the relationship between linguistic units and audio signals. Acoustic models are trained to recognize different sounds and phonemes in speech.

- Language Modeling: Language models predict the probability of word sequences, helping the system generate coherent and contextually appropriate transcriptions.

Impact of Speech Recognition:

Speech recognition systems are widely used in various applications such as virtual assistants, transcription services, and accessibility tools. For example, virtual assistants like

Google Assistant and Apple's Siri use speech recognition to understand and respond to voice commands. In transcription services, speech recognition is used to convert audio recordings into written text, saving time and effort in manual transcription.

Text Classification

Text classification involves categorizing texts into predefined classes or categories. NLP techniques are used to analyze the content of texts and assign them to appropriate categories based on their features and context.

Key Techniques in Text Classification:

- Rule-Based Methods: These methods use predefined rules and patterns to classify texts. While straightforward, they may not handle complex or ambiguous texts effectively.

- Machine Learning-Based Methods: Modern text classification systems use machine learning algorithms to train models on labeled datasets. These models can learn to classify texts based on features such as word frequency, context, and syntactic structure.

Impact of Text Classification

Text classification is used in various applications such as spam detection, sentiment analysis, and topic categorization. For instance, email systems use text classification to filter out spam messages. In sentiment analysis, text classification is used to determine the sentiment of reviews and social media posts. In content management, text classification helps organize and categorize large volumes of text data, making it easier to manage and retrieve information.

Natural Language Processing (NLP) is a dynamic and rapidly

evolving field that plays a crucial role in the interaction between computers and human language. By enabling computers to understand, interpret, and generate human language, NLP has revolutionized numerous applications across various domains. From language translation and sentiment analysis to chatbots and information retrieval, NLP has made significant contributions to enhancing the capabilities of AI systems and improving the overall user experience. As NLP continues to advance, it holds great promise for further transforming the way we interact with technology and access information.

Computer Vision:

- Definition: This subfield focuses on enabling machines to interpret and make decisions based on visual input from the world.

- Applications: Common applications include facial recognition, object detection, and autonomous driving.

Robotics:

- Definition: Robotics combines AI with engineering to create machines capable of performing physical tasks.

- Applications: Robots are used in manufacturing, healthcare, and space exploration.

Expert Systems:

- Definition: These systems emulate the decision-making abilities of a human expert.

- Components: Typically consist of a knowledge base and an inference engine. The knowledge base contains domain-specific knowledge, while the inference engine applies logical rules to this knowledge.

Reinforcement Learning:

- Definition: A type of machine learning where an agent learns to make decisions by performing actions and receiving feedback.

- Applications: Used in game playing, robotics, and certain

types of recommendation systems.

Fuzzy Logic:

- Definition: Unlike traditional binary logic, fuzzy logic deals with reasoning that is approximate rather than fixed and exact.

- Applications: Commonly used in control systems, such as those in household appliances and vehicle subsystems.

Natural Language Processing (NLP)

Natural Language Processing (NLP) is a critical area of AI focused on the interaction between computers and humans through natural language. The goal of NLP is to enable computers to understand, interpret, and generate human languages in a way that is both meaningful and useful.

NLP sits at the intersection of computer science, artificial intelligence, and linguistics, and it draws on methods and insights from each of these fields. The complexity of human language means that NLP is a challenging and multifaceted area of research and application. Here, we explore some of the core aspects of NLP, including its main tasks, techniques, and applications.

Core Tasks in NLP

Text Classification:

  - Definition: This involves categorizing text into predefined groups.

  - Applications: Spam detection in emails, sentiment analysis, and topic labeling.

Machine Translation:

  - Definition: The automatic translation of text or speech from one language to another.

  - Applications: Tools like Google Translate and multilingual customer service chatbots.

Named Entity Recognition (NER):

  - Definition: The process of identifying and classifying key elements (entities) in text into predefined categories such as names of people, organizations, locations, etc.

  - Applications: Information retrieval, content categorization, and enhancing search engines.

Part-of-Speech Tagging:

  - Definition: Assigning parts of speech to each word in a sentence, such as nouns, verbs, adjectives, etc.

  - Applications: Text-to-speech systems, grammatical checking tools, and syntactic parsing.

Sentiment Analysis:

  - Definition: Determining the sentiment or emotional tone behind a series of words, used to understand the attitudes, opinions, and emotions expressed.

- Applications: Social media monitoring, customer feedback analysis, and market research.

Speech Recognition:

- Definition: The process of converting spoken language into text.

- Applications: Voice-activated assistants like Siri and Alexa, transcription services, and hands-free computing.

Text Generation:

- Definition: Creating human-like text based on a given input.

- Applications: Automated content creation, chatbots, and story generation.

Coreference Resolution:

- Definition: Identifying when different words refer to the same entity in a text.

- Applications: Enhancing machine translation and improving question-answering systems.

Techniques in NLP

Tokenization:

- Definition: The process of breaking text into individual pieces, or tokens, which can be words, phrases, or symbols.

- Importance: It is the first step in many NLP tasks, enabling further analysis and processing.

Stemming and Lemmatization:

- Stemming: Reducing words to their base or root form.

- Lemmatization: Reducing words to their base or dictionary form, considering the context.

- Applications: Both are used in search engines and text analysis to treat different forms of a word as equivalent.

Parsing:

- Definition: Analyzing the grammatical structure of a sentence.

- Types: Can be syntactic (structure-focused) or semantic (meaning-focused).

- Applications: Important for machine translation and question-answering systems.

Word Embeddings:

- Definition: Representing words in a continuous vector space where similar words are located closer to each other.

- Examples: Word2Vec, GloVe, FastText.

- Applications: Used in almost all modern NLP applications, including language modeling and sentiment analysis.

Recurrent Neural Networks (RNNs) and Transformers:

- RNNs: A type of neural network designed to handle sequential data, where the output from previous steps is fed as input to the current step.

- Transformers: A more recent and powerful architecture that allows for parallel processing and improved handling of long-range dependencies.

- Applications: Both are used in machine translation, text generation, and more.

Attention Mechanisms:

- Definition: Techniques that allow models to focus on specific parts of the input sequence when generating the output.

- Applications: Key component in transformers, enhancing tasks like translation and summarization.

Applications of NLP

Virtual Assistants:

- Examples: Siri, Alexa, Google Assistant.

- Functionality: These systems use NLP to understand and respond to user queries, perform tasks, and provide information.

Chatbots:

- Usage: Used in customer service to handle inquiries, resolve issues, and provide information.

- Benefits: Enhance customer experience by providing instant responses and support.

Sentiment Analysis:

- Applications: Used by companies to gauge public opinion about products, services, or events.

- Tools: Social media monitoring tools often incorporate sentiment analysis to track and analyze customer sentiment.

Machine Translation:

 - Examples: Google Translate, DeepL.

 - Usage: Enables communication across language barriers, facilitates multilingual content creation.

Content Recommendation:

 - Applications: Online platforms like Netflix, Amazon, and YouTube use NLP to analyze user preferences and recommend relevant content.

 - Impact: Improves user engagement and satisfaction.

Healthcare:

 - Usage: NLP is used to extract valuable insights from unstructured medical records, assist in diagnosis, and enhance patient care.

 - Examples: Clinical decision support systems, automated summarization of patient notes.

Finance:

 - Applications: Fraud detection, sentiment analysis of

market news, and automated trading systems.

- Benefits: Enhances the accuracy and efficiency of financial operations.

Legal Tech:

- Usage: NLP is used to analyze legal documents, perform contract review, and assist with legal research.

- Impact: Saves time and reduces costs in legal proceedings. Artificial Intelligence and Natural Language Processing are transformative technologies with the potential to revolutionize numerous fields. AI, through its various subfields, aims to emulate and enhance human capabilities, while NLP focuses specifically on the intricate challenge of enabling machines to understand and generate human language. As these technologies continue to evolve, they will unlock new possibilities, drive innovation, and change the way we interact with machines and each other.

Chapter 2 History of Language Models

The history of language models, integral to the field of Natural Language Processing (NLP), is marked by a fascinating evolution from early rule-based systems to sophisticated statistical models, culminating in the advent of neural networks.

Rule-Based Systems

The earliest attempts at creating language models were primarily rule-based systems. These systems relied on handcrafted rules and extensive linguistic knowledge to process and generate language. In the 1950s and 1960s, linguists and computer scientists like Noam Chomsky laid the foundational work for these models with the development of formal grammars and syntax theories. Chomsky's transformational grammar, for instance, provided a framework for understanding the syntactic structures of language, which could be encoded into rules for language processing.

Rule-based systems typically involved a comprehensive set of if-then rules that described the syntax and sometimes the semantics of the target language. These rules were often derived from linguistic theories and required deep domain expertise. Early NLP applications such as machine translation systems (e.g., the Georgetown-IBM experiment in 1954) and simple chatbots like ELIZA (developed by Joseph Weizenbaum in the 1960s) used these rule-based approaches. While rule-based systems were groundbreaking, they had significant limitations. They were inflexible, difficult to scale, and heavily dependent on the quality and completeness of the rules. As language is inherently ambiguous and context-dependent, it was challenging to account for all possible variations and exceptions using fixed rules.

Statistical Models

The limitations of rule-based systems led to the exploration of statistical models in the 1980s and 1990s. Statistical models represented a paradigm shift in language processing, emphasizing data-driven approaches over handcrafted rules. The advent of more powerful computers and the availability of large corpora of text facilitated this transition. Statistical language models are based on the idea of probability distributions over sequences of words. The most fundamental statistical model is the n-gram model, which predicts the probability of a word based on the previous n-1 words. For example, a bigram model (n=2) considers the probability of a word given the preceding word, while a trigram model (n=3) extends this to the two preceding words. N-gram models were a significant improvement over rule-based systems because they could be trained on large datasets and capture the statistical properties of language. They were used in various NLP tasks such as speech recognition, machine translation, and text generation. However, n-gram models had their own set of challenges. They struggled with data sparsity, as the number of possible n-grams grows exponentially with n, making it difficult to estimate probabilities for rare or unseen n-grams. Moreover, they had limited ability to capture long-range dependencies in text. To address some of these issues, researchers developed more sophisticated statistical models. One notable advancement was the introduction of the Hidden Markov Model (HMM) for part-of-speech tagging and other sequence labeling tasks. HMMs use a probabilistic framework to model sequences of observations and hidden states, providing a way to incorporate contextual information.

Another significant development was the use of maximum entropy models and conditional random fields (CRFs). These models allowed for the integration of various features and contextual information in a more flexible manner than HMMs, improving performance on tasks such as named entity recognition and information extraction.

The Advent of Neural Networks in NLP

The real revolution in language modeling came with the advent of neural networks, particularly deep learning, in the late 2000s and 2010s. Neural networks offered a powerful and flexible framework for modeling complex patterns in language data, leading to significant advancements in NLP.

Early Neural Network Models

The application of neural networks to NLP began with simple feedforward neural networks and evolved into more sophisticated architectures. One of the early successes was the development of word embeddings, which represented words as dense vectors in a continuous space. Techniques like Word2Vec, introduced by Mikolov et al. in 2013, revolutionized NLP by capturing semantic relationships between words through unsupervised learning.

Word embeddings allowed models to generalize better across similar words and significantly improved the performance of various NLP tasks. However, these embeddings were static, meaning each word had a single representation regardless of context.

Recurrent Neural Networks (RNNs)

To better capture sequential information and context, researchers turned to Recurrent Neural Networks (RNNs). RNNs have a recursive structure that enables them to maintain a hidden state, effectively allowing them to remember previous inputs. This made RNNs well-suited for language modeling tasks where context and word order are crucial.

Despite their promise, standard RNNs struggled with learning long-range dependencies due to issues like vanishing and exploding gradients. This led to the development of more advanced RNN variants, such as Long Short-Term Memory (LSTM) networks and Gated Recurrent Units (GRUs). Introduced by Hochreiter and Schmidhuber in 1997, LSTMs used gating mechanisms to control the flow of information, making it easier to capture long-term dependencies in text.

GRUs, proposed by Cho et al. in 2014, simplified the LSTM architecture while retaining its ability to model long-range dependencies effectively.

LSTM and GRU networks became the backbone of many state-of-the-art NLP systems, achieving remarkable results in tasks like machine translation, speech recognition, and text generation.

The Attention Mechanism and Transformers

While RNNs represented a significant leap forward, they were not without limitations. Training RNNs, especially on long sequences, was computationally intensive, and they struggled with parallelization due to their sequential nature. The introduction of the attention mechanism by Bahdanau et al.

in 2014 addressed some of these challenges.

The attention mechanism allows the model to focus on different parts of the input sequence when generating each part of the output. This enables the model to capture relevant information from the entire input sequence, rather than relying solely on the hidden state. Attention mechanisms improved the performance of RNN-based models, particularly in machine translation.

The transformative moment in NLP came with the introduction of the Transformer model by Vaswani et al. in 2017. The Transformer architecture dispensed with recurrence entirely, relying solely on self-attention mechanisms to process input sequences. This innovation allowed for greater parallelization during training, significantly speeding up the training process and enabling the modeling of longer dependencies in text.

The Transformer model consists of an encoder-decoder

architecture, where both the encoder and decoder are composed of multiple layers of self-attention and feedforward neural networks. Transformers quickly became the foundation for state-of-the-art language models, leading to breakthroughs in various NLP tasks.

Pre-trained Language Models

Building on the success of Transformers, researchers developed pre-trained language models that could be fine-tuned for specific tasks. The idea was to pre-train a model on a large corpus of text using unsupervised learning objectives, such as language modeling or masked language modeling, and then fine-tune the model on task-specific data.

One of the earliest and most influential pre-trained models was BERT (Bidirectional Encoder Representations from Transformers), introduced by Devlin et al. in 2018. BERT uses a masked language modeling objective to pre-train the model on large text corpora, capturing bidirectional context for each word. This bidirectional context allows BERT to understand the meaning of words based on both their left and right context, improving performance on a wide range of NLP tasks.

Following BERT, numerous pre-trained models have been developed, each pushing the boundaries of what is possible in NLP. Notable examples include GPT (Generative Pre-trained Transformer) by OpenAI, which uses a unidirectional language modeling objective for pre-training, and T5 (Text-To-Text Transfer Transformer) by Google, which frames all NLP tasks as text-to-text transformations.

GPT-3, introduced by OpenAI in 2020, represents one of the most advanced language models to date, with 175 billion parameters. GPT-3 demonstrated impressive capabilities in generating human-like text, performing few-shot learning, and even solving complex tasks with minimal instruction.

The evolution of language models from rule-based systems to statistical models, and ultimately to neural networks, reflects the broader trends in artificial intelligence and machine learning. Each stage of this evolution has brought significant advancements, addressing the limitations of previous approaches and pushing the boundaries of what is possible in NLP.

Rule-based systems laid the groundwork for understanding the syntactic and semantic structures of language, but their rigidity and reliance on handcrafted rules limited their scalability. Statistical models introduced data-driven approaches, enabling the capture of language patterns through probability distributions. However, they struggled with data sparsity and long-range dependencies.

The advent of neural networks, particularly deep learning and the Transformer architecture, revolutionized NLP by providing powerful, flexible, and scalable models that can learn complex patterns from large datasets. Pre-trained language models have further democratized NLP, allowing for rapid development and deployment of state-of-the-art models across a wide range of applications.

As we look to the future, the ongoing research in neural network architectures, unsupervised learning, and transfer learning promises to further advance the field of NLP, enabling even more sophisticated and capable language models.

Chapter 3 What are Large Language Models

Large Language Models (LLMs) are a type of artificial intelligence (AI) that are designed to understand, generate, and manipulate human language at an advanced level. They are based on deep learning architectures, typically neural networks, that are trained on vast amounts of text data. The training process involves adjusting the parameters of the model to predict the next word in a sentence, given the preceding words. This process, repeated over billions of words, allows the model to learn the statistical properties of language.

LLMs fall under the broader category of Natural Language Processing (NLP), which encompasses a range of technologies aimed at enabling machines to interpret and interact with human language. However, what distinguishes LLMs is their size and complexity. The term "large" refers not only to the amount of data they are trained on but also to the number of parameters they contain. These models often have hundreds of billions of parameters, making them capable of capturing subtle nuances and complex patterns in language.

Key Characteristics and Capabilities

- Scale and Complexity

The sheer scale of LLMs is one of their defining

characteristics. Models like GPT-3, developed by OpenAI, contain 175 billion parameters. The training data for these models includes a diverse range of texts from books, websites, and other textual resources. This extensive training allows LLMs to generalize across various topics and styles of writing. The complexity of these models enables them to perform a wide array of language-related tasks, often surpassing previous state-of-the-art methods.

- Language Understanding

LLMs exhibit a profound understanding of language. This understanding is not just superficial but extends to the comprehension of context, syntax, semantics, and even pragmatic aspects of language use. They can interpret and generate text that is coherent and contextually appropriate, making them useful for tasks such as translation, summarization, and question-answering. The ability to understand and generate human-like text allows LLMs to engage in meaningful conversations with users, providing responses that are relevant and informative.

- Text Generation

One of the most remarkable capabilities of LLMs is text generation. Given a prompt, these models can produce coherent and contextually relevant text that can range from a few sentences to entire articles. This capability is utilized in various applications, including creative writing, content creation, and automated report generation. The quality of the generated text can often be indistinguishable from that written by humans, demonstrating the advanced linguistic capabilities of these models.

- Contextual Awareness

LLMs have the ability to maintain contextual awareness over extended passages of text. This means they can keep track of the topic, characters, and events mentioned earlier in a conversation or document, enabling them to produce more coherent and contextually appropriate responses. This characteristic is particularly important in applications such as dialogue systems and chatbots, where maintaining the context of a conversation is crucial for providing relevant and accurate responses.

- Adaptability and Transfer Learning

Another key capability of LLMs is their adaptability. These models can be fine-tuned for specific tasks or domains with relatively small amounts of additional training data. This process, known as transfer learning, leverages the knowledge acquired during the initial training phase and adapts it to new tasks. This makes LLMs highly versatile, capable of performing a wide range of language-related tasks with minimal additional training.

- Multimodal Capabilities

Recent advancements have extended the capabilities of LLMs beyond text to include multimodal inputs, such as images and speech. Models like GPT-4 and others incorporate these capabilities, allowing them to process and generate content that integrates text with other media forms. This opens up new possibilities for applications in fields such as virtual assistants, educational tools, and interactive storytelling, where a combination of text, images, and audio can provide a richer user experience.

Applications of Large Language Models

- Natural Language Understanding and Processing

LLMs are at the forefront of advancements in natural language understanding (NLU) and processing. They are used in applications such as sentiment analysis, where they analyze the sentiment expressed in a piece of text, and named entity recognition (NER), where they identify and classify entities mentioned in the text. These capabilities are essential for various industries, including finance, healthcare, and customer service, where understanding the content and context of textual data is crucial.

- Conversational Agents and Chatbots

The ability of LLMs to generate coherent and contextually appropriate text makes them ideal for creating conversational agents and chatbots. These systems can engage in natural and meaningful conversations with users, providing information, answering questions, and assisting with tasks. In customer service, chatbots powered by LLMs can handle a large volume of inquiries, improving efficiency and customer satisfaction. In healthcare, they can provide preliminary medical advice and triage, assisting both patients and healthcare professionals.

Content Creation and Curation

LLMs are increasingly used in content creation and curation. They can generate articles, reports, and creative writing pieces, aiding writers and journalists in producing content more efficiently. In marketing, they can create personalized and engaging content for campaigns, improving audience engagement. Furthermore, LLMs can curate content by summarizing large volumes of text, extracting key information, and presenting it in a concise and readable format.

Translation and Multilingual Applications

The ability of LLMs to understand and generate text in multiple languages makes them powerful tools for translation and multilingual applications. They can provide high-quality translations that capture the nuances of the source text, facilitating communication across language barriers.

Additionally, they can be used to create multilingual content, ensuring that information is accessible to a global audience.

Education and Training

In education, LLMs can serve as tutors, providing personalized instruction and feedback to students. They can assist with language learning by engaging students in conversations and correcting their mistakes. Furthermore, they can generate educational materials, such as quizzes and exercises, tailored to the needs of individual learners. In corporate training, LLMs can create customized training programs and materials, enhancing the learning experience for employees.

Research and Data Analysis

LLMs are valuable tools for researchers and analysts. They can process and analyze large volumes of text data, identifying patterns, trends, and insights that would be difficult to uncover manually. In fields such as social sciences and humanities, they can assist with textual analysis, sentiment analysis, and discourse analysis. In scientific research, they can help with literature reviews, extracting relevant information from research papers and summarizing key findings.

Challenges

Despite their remarkable capabilities, LLMs present several challenges and ethical considerations.

1. Bias and Fairness

LLMs can inadvertently learn and perpetuate biases present in their training data. This can result in biased or unfair outputs, particularly in sensitive applications such as hiring or lending. Addressing these biases is a significant challenge, requiring careful selection and curation of training data, as well as ongoing monitoring and evaluation of the model's outputs.

2. Transparency and Explainability

The complexity of LLMs makes it difficult to understand and explain how they arrive at their outputs. This lack of transparency can be problematic, particularly in applications where accountability and trust are crucial. Developing methods to interpret and explain the decision-making processes of LLMs is an active area of research, aimed at making these models more transparent and trustworthy.

3. Data Privacy and Security

The training and deployment of LLMs involve handling large amounts of data, raising concerns about data privacy and security. Ensuring that the data used to train these models is collected and used ethically, and that the models themselves do not inadvertently leak sensitive information, is essential for maintaining user trust and compliance with data protection regulations.

4. Resource Consumption

Training and deploying LLMs require significant computational resources, leading to concerns about their environmental impact and accessibility. Efforts are underway to develop more efficient training methods and architectures, reducing the resource consumption of LLMs and making them more accessible to a wider range of users and organizations.

Future Directions

The future of LLMs holds exciting possibilities, driven by ongoing advancements in AI research and technology.

1. Improved Efficiency and Accessibility

Researchers are developing more efficient algorithms and architectures, reducing the computational resources required for training and deployment. This will make LLMs more accessible to a broader range of users and applications, democratizing the benefits of this technology.

2. Enhanced Multimodal Capabilities

Future LLMs are likely to incorporate even more advanced

multimodal capabilities, integrating text, images, audio, and other forms of data seamlessly. This will enable the creation of richer and more interactive applications, enhancing user experiences across various domains.

3. Responsible AI

The development of ethical and responsible AI practices will continue to be a priority. This includes addressing issues of bias and fairness, improving transparency and explainability, and ensuring data privacy and security. Establishing robust guidelines and standards for the ethical use of LLMs will be crucial for their responsible deployment.

4. Personalization and Adaptability

Future LLMs will become even more personalized and adaptable, capable of tailoring their outputs to individual users' needs and preferences. This will enhance their effectiveness in applications such as education, healthcare, and customer service, providing more personalized and relevant experiences.

Large Language Models represent a significant advancement in the field of artificial intelligence, offering unprecedented capabilities in understanding, generating, and interacting with human language. Their scale and complexity enable them to perform a wide range of language-related tasks, from text generation and translation to content creation and conversational agents. However, their deployment also presents challenges and ethical considerations that must be addressed to ensure their responsible and beneficial use. As research and development in this field continue, LLMs are poised to become even more powerful and versatile tools, transforming the way we interact with technology and each other.

Chapter 4 Applications of LLMs

Large Language Models (LLMs) represent a significant advancement in the field of artificial intelligence (AI) and natural language processing (NLP). These models, such as GPT-4 developed by OpenAI, have the capability to understand and generate human-like text, making them incredibly versatile tools. This essay explores the real-world applications of LLMs and their impacts across various industries.

Real-World Applications of LLMs

1. Customer Support and Chatbots:

One of the most prevalent applications of LLMs is in customer support. Companies leverage LLMs to create intelligent chatbots that can handle customer queries efficiently. These chatbots can understand context, respond in natural language, and even escalate issues to human agents when necessary. This not only enhances customer experience but also reduces operational costs.

2. Content Creation and Media:

LLMs are revolutionizing content creation across media and publishing industries. They can generate articles, create marketing copy, draft reports, and even write books. For instance, tools like Jasper and Copy.ai use LLMs to help marketers generate ad copy and social media posts. This automation allows writers to focus on more creative and

85

strategic tasks.

3. Education and E-Learning:

In the educational sector, LLMs are used to create personalized learning experiences. They can generate customized educational materials, provide explanations, and answer student queries. Furthermore, LLMs can assist in grading by evaluating written assignments and providing feedback, thus saving educators significant time.

4. Healthcare:

The healthcare industry benefits from LLMs in various ways. They can assist in the documentation process by transcribing and summarizing patient notes, which allows healthcare professionals to focus more on patient care. Additionally, LLMs can provide preliminary diagnostics by analyzing patient data and suggesting possible conditions, which can be further validated by doctors.

5. Legal and Compliance:

Legal professionals use LLMs to analyze large volumes of documents, draft contracts, and perform legal research. LLMs can identify relevant case laws and statutes, thus expediting the research process. They can also help ensure compliance by monitoring regulatory changes and alerting businesses to necessary adaptations.

6. Translation and Localization:

LLMs have significantly improved the quality of machine translation. Services like Google Translate use LLMs to provide more accurate and contextually appropriate translations. This is crucial for businesses operating in multiple countries, as it ensures that marketing materials, user manuals, and other documents are accurately localized.

7. Finance and Banking:

In finance, LLMs assist in various functions such as analyzing market trends, generating reports, and providing customer support. They can process vast amounts of data to detect fraudulent activities, predict market movements, and even manage personal finances through intelligent financial advisors.

8. Entertainment and Gaming:

The entertainment industry uses LLMs to create engaging content. In gaming, LLMs can generate dynamic dialogues and narratives, providing a more immersive experience. They can also be used to script virtual influencers and interactive storylines, making content more engaging.

Impacts on Various Industries

1. Retail and E-commerce:

LLMs are transforming the retail and e-commerce sectors by enhancing customer interaction and personalizing shopping experiences. Chatbots powered by LLMs can recommend products based on customer preferences and previous purchases. Additionally, LLMs can analyze customer reviews and feedback to help businesses improve their products and services.

2. Manufacturing:

In manufacturing, LLMs contribute to optimizing operations by analyzing production data and predicting maintenance needs. They can streamline supply chain management by forecasting demand and managing inventory. This leads to reduced downtime and increased efficiency.

3. Telecommunications:

The telecommunications industry utilizes LLMs to enhance customer service, manage network performance, and provide personalized services. By analyzing customer data, telecom companies can offer targeted plans and services, improving customer satisfaction and retention.

4. Transportation and Logistics:

LLMs improve logistics by optimizing routes and predicting delivery times. They can analyze traffic patterns and weather conditions to suggest the most efficient routes, thus reducing fuel consumption and operational costs. In public transportation, LLMs can provide real-time updates and customer service through chatbots.

5. Energy Sector:

In the energy sector, LLMs help in monitoring and

optimizing the performance of power plants and grids. They can predict equipment failures and suggest preventive maintenance. Additionally, LLMs can analyze energy consumption patterns to help companies implement more efficient energy management practices.

6. Marketing and Advertising:

Marketing and advertising heavily rely on LLMs for consumer insights and targeted campaigns. By analyzing social media trends and consumer behavior, LLMs can help marketers create highly personalized and effective campaigns. They also assist in A/B testing and optimizing ad performance in real time.

7. Human Resources:

In HR, LLMs streamline recruitment by screening resumes and conducting initial candidate interviews. They can also be used to analyze employee feedback and engagement, helping HR professionals to improve workplace culture and productivity. Moreover, LLMs can assist in drafting HR policies and compliance documents.

8. Real Estate:

The real estate industry benefits from LLMs through enhanced property management and customer service. LLMs can analyze market trends to provide insights into property values and investment opportunities. They also help real estate agents by automating tasks such as scheduling viewings and answering client queries.

9. Travel and Hospitality:

In travel and hospitality, LLMs enhance the customer experience by providing personalized travel recommendations and managing bookings. They can analyze customer preferences and past behavior to suggest travel itineraries and accommodations. Additionally, LLMs power chatbots that assist travelers with real-time information and support.

10. Public Sector and Government:

Government agencies use LLMs to improve public services and citizen engagement. They can automate the processing of forms and applications, provide information through chatbots, and analyze data to inform policy decisions. In law enforcement, LLMs assist in crime analysis and prediction, enhancing public safety.

The importance and applications of Large Language Models (LLMs) are vast and ever-growing. Their ability to understand and generate human-like text makes them invaluable tools across numerous industries. From enhancing customer support to revolutionizing content creation, education, healthcare, and beyond, LLMs are driving significant advancements and efficiencies. Their impact on industries such as retail, manufacturing, telecommunications, transportation, energy, marketing, human resources, real estate, travel, and the public sector is profound, enabling better decision-making, personalized services, and optimized operations.

As LLMs continue to evolve, their applications and impacts will expand further, potentially transforming even more aspects of our daily lives and professional environments. The integration of LLMs into various sectors not only highlights the importance of continued research and development in this field but also underscores the need for ethical considerations to ensure that these powerful tools are used responsibly and for the greater good.

Chapter 5 Basics of Neural Networks

Neural networks are a fundamental concept in artificial intelligence and machine learning, inspired by the biological neural networks of the human brain. They are powerful tools for solving complex problems in pattern recognition, classification, regression, and more. In this discussion, we'll explore the foundational elements of neural networks: neurons, layers, and activation functions.

Neurons

Neurons are the basic building blocks of a neural network.

Each neuron is a computational unit that takes one or more inputs, processes them, and produces an output. In biological terms, neurons receive signals from dendrites, process these signals in the cell body (soma), and transmit the output signal through the axon to other neurons.

In artificial neural networks (ANNs), a neuron (or node) receives input signals from the previous layer (or directly from the input data in the case of the first layer), computes a weighted sum of these inputs, and applies an activation function to determine the output of the neuron. Mathematically, the output y of a neuron can be represented as:

$$y = f \left(\sum_{i-1}^{n} w_i x_i + b \right)$$

where:

- x_i are the inputs to the neuron,

- w_i are the weights associated with each input,

- b is the bias term,

- f is the activation function.

Layers

Neurons are organized into layers in a neural network. A typical neural network consists of three main types of layers: input layer, hidden layers, and output layer.

1. Input Layer: This layer receives the initial input data and passes it on to the next layer. Each neuron in the input layer represents a feature or attribute of the input data.

2. Hidden Layers: These layers are between the input and output layers and perform computations to transform the input into something that the output layer can use. Each

hidden layer typically contains multiple neurons that process information in parallel.

3. Output Layer: The final layer of neurons produces the output of the neural network. The number of neurons in the output layer depends on the type of problem being solved. For example, in a binary classification task, there might be one neuron in the output layer representing the probability of one class, while the probability of the other class is implicitly given by $(1 - \text{output})$.

Activation Functions

Activation functions introduce non-linearity into the output of a neuron. This non-linearity is crucial for enabling neural networks to model complex relationships in data. Some commonly used activation functions include:

1. **Sigmoid Function**: $\sigma(z) = \frac{1}{1+e^{-z}}$, where z is the weighted sum of inputs. It squashes the output to a range between 0 and 1, which is useful for binary classification tasks.

2. **Hyperbolic Tangent (Tanh) Function**: $\tanh(z) = \frac{e^z - e^{-z}}{e^z + e^{-z}}$. Similar to the sigmoid function, but squashes the output to a range between -1 and 1, which can make training neural networks easier.

3. **Rectified Linear Unit (ReLU)**: $\mathrm{ReLU}(z) = \max(0, z)$. It outputs zero if the input is negative, and otherwise, it outputs the input itself. ReLU is the most commonly used activation function in hidden layers due to its simplicity and effectiveness in training deep neural networks.

4. **Softmax Function**: This activation function is used in the output layer for multi-class classification tasks. It converts the raw output scores into probabilities that sum up to 1, making it easier to interpret which class the model predicts.

Training Neural Networks

Training a neural network involves optimizing the weights and biases of the neurons so that the network learns to map input data to the correct output. This process typically involves the following steps:

1. Forward Propagation: Compute the output of the neural network by propagating the input data forward through the

network, layer by layer.

2. Loss Calculation: Measure how far the network's predictions are from the actual target values using a loss function (e.g., mean squared error for regression tasks or cross-entropy loss for classification tasks).

3. Backward Propagation (Backpropagation): Propagate the error backward through the network to calculate the gradient of the loss function with respect to each weight and bias.

4. Gradient Descent: Adjust the weights and biases in the direction that minimizes the loss function gradient, typically using optimization techniques such as stochastic gradient descent (SGD) or its variants (e.g., Adam).

5. Repeat: Iterate through the dataset multiple times (epochs) to improve the network's performance until the model converges to a satisfactory solution.

Neural networks, with their neurons, layers, and activation functions, form the backbone of modern machine learning and AI applications. Understanding these fundamental components is essential for building and training effective neural network models that can solve a wide range of complex problems in various domains. As research continues to advance, neural networks are likely to play an even more significant role in shaping the future of artificial intelligence.

Chapter 6 Types of Neural Networks

Neural networks are foundational tools in modern machine learning and artificial intelligence, designed to mimic the workings of the human brain to process complex patterns and solve intricate tasks. Over the years, various types of neural networks have been developed, each tailored to specific types of data and tasks. This article explores three fundamental types of neural networks: feedforward, recurrent, and convolutional neural networks (CNNs). It delves into their architectures, applications, strengths, and limitations, highlighting their distinct roles in the landscape of AI and machine learning.

Feedforward Neural Networks (FNNs)

Feedforward neural networks are the simplest form of artificial neural networks, where information flows in one direction: forward, from input nodes through hidden nodes (if any) to output nodes. These networks are characterized by their layered structure, with each layer comprising a set of nodes (neurons) interconnected with the next layer but having no connections that form cycles.

Architecture and Working Mechanism

- Input Layer: This layer receives the initial data or features.
- Hidden Layers: Intermediate layers between the input and output layers, where the processing of data occurs through weighted connections and activation functions.
- Output Layer: The final layer that produces the network's predictions or classifications based on the processed

information.

Applications:

- Classification: Commonly used for tasks such as image recognition, text classification, and sentiment analysis.

- Regression: Predicting continuous values, such as stock prices or housing prices.

- Pattern Recognition: Identifying complex patterns in data.

Strengths:

- Simplicity: Easy to understand and implement.

- Universal Approximation: Capable, in theory, of approximating any continuous function given enough neurons and layers.

- Scalability: Can handle large datasets efficiently with parallel computing.

Limitations:

- Limited Contextual Understanding: Lacks memory of previous inputs, making them less effective for sequential data.

- Overfitting: Prone to overfitting with complex datasets without appropriate regularization techniques.

- Feature Engineering Dependency: Performance heavily reliant on feature selection and engineering.

Recurrent Neural Networks (RNNs)

Recurrent neural networks are designed to effectively model sequential data by maintaining a form of memory of previous inputs through hidden states. This memory enables RNNs to exhibit dynamic temporal behavior, making them suitable for tasks involving sequential dependencies and time-series data.

Architecture and Working Mechanism

- Recurrent Connections: Connections between nodes in the same layer that allow information to persist.

- Hidden State: Represents the network's memory, updated at each time step to incorporate current input and previous state.

- Output: Produced based on the current input and the updated hidden state.

Applications:

- Natural Language Processing (NLP): Tasks such as language modeling, machine translation, and text generation.

- Time-Series Prediction: Forecasting stock prices, weather patterns, or any sequential data.

- Speech Recognition: Converting audio signals into text.

Strengths:

- Sequential Data Handling: Effective in capturing dependencies across time steps.

- Flexibility: Can handle inputs of varying lengths.

- State Persistence: Maintains memory of previous inputs, enabling context awareness.

Limitations:

- Vanishing/Exploding Gradient Problem: Gradient instability during training can hinder learning long-term dependencies.

- Computational Intensity: More complex than feedforward networks, leading to slower training times.

- Short-Term Memory Limitation: Difficulty in retaining information over long sequences due to inherent design constraints.

Convolutional Neural Networks (CNNs)

Convolutional neural networks are specialized for processing grid-like data, such as images or sound waves, where the architecture takes advantage of the spatial nature of the input. CNNs use convolutional layers to automatically learn hierarchical representations of the input data, making them highly effective for tasks involving spatial relationships and local patterns.

Architecture and Working Mechanism

- Convolutional Layers: Apply filters (kernels) over input data to extract local features.

- Pooling Layers: Aggregate extracted features to reduce spatial dimensions and computational complexity.

- Fully Connected Layers: Process flattened features for final classification or regression.

Applications:

- Image Recognition: Classifying objects within images, object detection, and facial recognition.

- Computer Vision Tasks: Segmentation, optical character recognition (OCR), and image generation.

- Natural Language Processing: Text classification based on

word embeddings.

Strengths:

- Spatial Hierarchical Learning: Effective in capturing spatial dependencies within data.

- Parameter Sharing: Reduces the number of parameters by sharing weights across the input, improving efficiency.

- Translation Invariance: Capability to recognize features regardless of their position in the input.

Limitations:

- Data Efficiency: Require large amounts of labeled data for effective training.

- Computational Intensity: More complex architectures can be computationally expensive.

- Interpretability: Understanding how CNNs arrive at decisions can be challenging due to their layered and hierarchical structure.

Each type of neural network—feedforward, recurrent, and convolutional—comes with its unique architecture, strengths, and limitations, making them suitable for different types of data and tasks in machine learning and AI. Feedforward networks excel in straightforward data processing tasks, while recurrent networks handle sequential data with memory, and convolutional networks specialize in spatially structured data like images. As advancements continue, hybrid architectures and specialized variants of these networks are emerging, further expanding the capabilities and applications of neural networks across various domains. Understanding these distinctions is crucial for effectively applying neural networks to real-world problems and advancing the field of artificial intelligence.

Chapter 7 Transformers

Transformers have revolutionized the field of Natural Language Processing (NLP) since their introduction, representing a significant breakthrough in how machines understand and generate human language. This technology has enabled unprecedented advancements in various NLP tasks, surpassing previous models in both efficiency and effectiveness. This article explores the foundational aspects of transformers, beginning with their breakthrough in NLP and delving into their detailed architecture.

The Breakthrough of Transformers in NLP

Before transformers, recurrent neural networks (RNNs) and

convolutional neural networks (CNNs) dominated the NLP landscape. However, these models faced challenges in capturing long-range dependencies in text and scaling effectively to larger datasets. Transformers, introduced by Vaswani et al. in the seminal paper "Attention is All You Need" in 2017, offered a novel architecture that addressed these limitations.

One of the key breakthroughs of transformers lies in their attention mechanism. Unlike RNNs and CNNs, which process inputs sequentially or through local receptive fields, transformers leverage self-attention to weigh the importance of different words in a sentence. This mechanism allows transformers to consider all words simultaneously, capturing dependencies regardless of their distance apart. This capability significantly enhances the model's ability to understand context and improve performance on a wide range of NLP tasks, including language translation, sentiment analysis, and text generation.

Furthermore, transformers introduced the concept of "positional encodings" to maintain the sequential order of words, ensuring the model understands the relative positions of tokens within a sequence. This innovation contributed to transformers' success in processing variable-length inputs efficiently, a task that was challenging for previous architectures.

The transformer architecture not only achieved state-of-the-art results but also laid the groundwork for subsequent advancements such as BERT (Bidirectional Encoder Representations from Transformers), GPT (Generative Pre-trained Transformer), and T5 (Text-to-Text Transfer Transformer). These models further pushed the boundaries of NLP performance, demonstrating the enduring impact of transformers on the field.

Detailed Architecture of Transformers

The architecture of transformers comprises several key components that work together to process and understand textual data. Understanding these components is crucial for grasping how transformers operate and achieve their remarkable performance.

1. Self-Attention Mechanism: At the heart of the transformer architecture is the self-attention mechanism. This mechanism allows the model to weigh the significance of each word in the input sequence concerning every other word. Given an input sequence $X = (x_1, x_2, ..., x_n)$, where n is the sequence length, self-attention computes a set of attention scores A that determine how much each word should focus on the others. These scores are calculated using queries, keys, and values derived from the input embeddings.

- Query, Key, and Value: Each word in the sequence is transformed into three vectors: a query vector Q, a key vector K, and a value vector V. These vectors are learned during the training process and used to compute attention scores.

- Attention Scores: The attention score A_{ij} between word i and word j is computed as the dot product of the query of word i and the key of word j, scaled by a factor to stabilize gradients. Softmax normalization is applied to obtain the final attention weights.

- Weighted Sum: The weighted sum of the values V using the attention scores A produces the output of the self-attention layer. This output captures the contextual information of each word in relation to the entire input sequence.

2. Multi-Head Attention: To enhance the model's ability to focus on different parts of the input, transformers use multi-

head attention. This involves performing multiple parallel self-attention operations, each with its own set of queries, keys, and values. The outputs of these operations are concatenated and linearly transformed to obtain the final output of the multi-head attention layer.

3. Feedforward Neural Networks: After the attention mechanisms, transformers employ feedforward neural networks (FFNs) to process the outputs of the attention layers. FFNs consist of two linear transformations with a ReLU activation function in between. This component introduces non-linearity and allows the model to learn complex mappings between the input and output.

4. Layer Normalization and Residual Connections: Each sub-layer (attention and FFN) in the transformer architecture is followed by layer normalization, which normalizes the outputs across the feature dimension. Additionally, residual connections around each sub-layer facilitate gradient flow

during training and help mitigate the vanishing gradient problem.

5. Positional Encoding: Since transformers do not inherently encode the sequential order of words, positional encodings are added to the input embeddings to convey their positions in the sequence. Positional encodings are typically sine and cosine functions of different frequencies to provide a unique positional signal for each word.

6. Encoder-Decoder Architecture: In sequence-to-sequence tasks such as machine translation, transformers utilize an encoder-decoder architecture. The encoder processes the input sequence to generate a representation, while the decoder uses this representation to generate an output sequence. The decoder also incorporates an additional masked self-attention mechanism to ensure each position can only attend to previous positions during training.

7. Training and Optimization: Transformers are trained using variants of stochastic gradient descent (SGD) such as Adam, along with techniques like learning rate schedules and warm-up steps to stabilize training. Pre-training on large corpora followed by fine-tuning on task-specific data has become a common practice to achieve state-of-the-art results in NLP.

Transformers have emerged as a cornerstone technology in NLP, fundamentally altering how machines process and understand human language. Their attention-based architecture allows them to capture intricate linguistic patterns and long-range dependencies, surpassing previous models in both performance and scalability. As transformers continue to evolve with innovations like BERT, GPT, and beyond, they promise to drive further advancements in natural language understanding and generation. Understanding the architecture and breakthrough of transformers is crucial for anyone interested in the cutting-edge developments of NLP and AI.

Transformers represent a watershed moment in the field of NLP, embodying a paradigm shift towards attention mechanisms and parallel computation. Their impact is not only felt in academic research but also in practical applications across industries, paving the way for more sophisticated and context-aware AI systems.

Chapter 8 The Attention Mechanism

In recent years, the attention mechanism has revolutionized the field of natural language processing (NLP) and machine learning, particularly through its pivotal role in transformer models. This essay delves into the intricate workings of attention, exploring self-attention, its significance, and the evolution to multi-head attention within transformers.

Understanding Self-Attention

At its essence, self-attention is a mechanism that enables a model to weigh the significance of different parts of an input sequence. Initially introduced in the context of sequence-to-sequence learning and neural machine translation, self-attention allows the model to focus on relevant tokens within the input sequence while constructing representations that capture dependencies between elements.

Mechanics of Self-Attention

Self-attention operates by computing a weighted sum of values, where the weights are determined by the compatibility (similarity) between a query and keys derived from the input sequence. This can be mathematically expressed as:

$$\text{Attention}(Q, K, V) = \text{softmax}\left(\frac{QK^T}{\sqrt{d_k}}\right) V$$

Here,

- Q, K, and V represent the query, key, and value matrices respectively, derived from the input sequence.
- d_k is the dimensionality of the keys.
- softmax ensures that the weights sum to 1, determining the contribution of each value vector V to the output.

The output of self-attention provides a weighted combination of values, where tokens that are more relevant to the context encoded in the query are assigned higher weights.

Importance of Self-Attention

Self-attention's importance lies in its ability to capture long-range dependencies within sequences efficiently. Unlike traditional recurrent neural networks (RNNs) or convolutional neural networks (CNNs), which have difficulty in capturing dependencies beyond a fixed context window, self-attention can relate any two positions in the input sequence to compute the representation of each position. This makes it particularly effective for tasks involving long-term dependencies, such as machine translation, sentiment analysis, and document classification.

Furthermore, self-attention supports parallelization because computations for different positions in the sequence can be performed independently. This parallelism significantly accelerates training and inference times, making self-attention not only effective but also computationally efficient.

Multi-Head Attention and Its Role in Transformers

While self-attention forms the core of attention mechanisms, multi-head attention enhances its capabilities by allowing the model to jointly attend to information from different representation subspaces at different positions. Introduced in the transformer architecture, multi-head attention enables the model to learn diverse, context-aware representations, leading to improved performance on various NLP tasks.

Concept of Multi-Head Attention

In multi-head attention, the key, query, and value matrices are projected into multiple, lower-dimensional subspaces. This is achieved by splitting the matrices and computing attention in each subspace independently. The outputs from each attention head are then concatenated and linearly transformed to produce the final output.

Mathematically, multi-head attention can be defined as follows:

$$\text{MultiHead}(Q, K, V) = \text{Concat}(\text{head}_1, \ldots, \text{head}_h)W^O$$

where each head_i is computed as:

$$\text{head}_i = \text{Attention}(QW_i^Q, KW_i^K, VW_i^V)$$

Here,

- W_i^Q, W_i^K, and W_i^V are weight matrices for the query, key, and value projections of the i-th head.
- W^O is a weight matrix used to linearly combine the outputs of all heads.

Benefits of Multi-Head Attention

Multi-head attention enhances the expressiveness and

robustness of the model in several ways:

- Diverse Representations: Each attention head can focus on different aspects of the input sequence, allowing the model to capture various types of relationships and patterns.

- Improved Generalization: By learning multiple attention distributions, the model can generalize better across different tasks and datasets.

- Interpretable Attention: The outputs from different heads provide insights into which parts of the input are considered important for different aspects of the task, aiding interpretability.

Moreover, multi-head attention facilitates better gradient flow during training, which is crucial for deep neural networks. By attending to multiple representations simultaneously, the model can effectively manage and combine information across different levels of abstraction, leading to improved performance on complex NLP tasks such as question answering, language modeling, and summarization. The attention mechanism, with its evolution from self-attention to multi-head attention, has emerged as a cornerstone of modern deep learning architectures, particularly transformers. Its ability to capture dependencies across sequences and to learn diverse representations has propelled advancements in natural language understanding and generation tasks. As research continues to refine and extend the capabilities of attention mechanisms, the transformative impact on AI applications is poised to grow, promising further breakthroughs in language understanding, reasoning, and beyond.

Chapter 9 Encoder-Decoder Architecture

In deep learning and neural networks, the encoder-decoder architecture has emerged as a pivotal framework for various tasks such as machine translation, image captioning, and speech recognition. This chapter delves into the fundamental aspects of encoder-decoder architecture, exploring its structure, functions of the encoder and decoder components, and the distinctions between different configurations: encoder-only, decoder-only, and full encoder-decoder models.

Structure and Function of Encoder-Decoder Architecture

The encoder-decoder architecture consists of two main components: the encoder and the decoder. Each component plays a crucial role in processing input data and generating meaningful outputs. Let's explore their structures and functions in detail:

Encoder

- Structure: The encoder typically comprises one or more layers of neural networks, such as convolutional layers in the case of image data or recurrent layers for sequential data like text or speech. These layers are designed to extract relevant features from the input data.

- Function: Its primary function is to transform the input data (e.g., an image, sentence, or audio waveform) into a fixed-dimensional representation called a context vector or latent representation. This representation captures the essential information of the input in a compressed form, which is crucial for subsequent tasks performed by the decoder.

Decoder

- Structure: The decoder is another set of neural network layers, often designed to be symmetric to the encoder. It takes the context vector generated by the encoder and generates the desired output based on this representation.

- Function: The main function of the decoder is to generate output sequences or structures that are relevant to the input. For instance, in machine translation, the decoder would take the latent representation of the source sentence and generate the corresponding translated sentence in the target language.

Working Together

- The encoder and decoder work in tandem: the encoder processes the input to derive a meaningful representation, and the decoder uses this representation to generate the desired output. This process is iterative and involves training the entire architecture to optimize both components for the specific task at hand.

Differences Between Encoder-Only, Decoder-Only, and Full Encoder-Decoder Models

While the basic encoder-decoder architecture describes a system with both encoder and decoder components, variations exist depending on how these components are used:

1. Encoder-Only Models:

- Definition: Encoder-only models, also known as feature extraction models, consist solely of the encoder component.

- Function: These models are used to extract meaningful features from the input data. The context vectors generated by the encoder can be used as input to other systems or models for further processing.

- Example Application: In image processing, an encoder-only model can be used to extract features from images for tasks like image classification or object detection without requiring a decoder for generating outputs.

2. Decoder-Only Models:

- Definition: Decoder-only models focus solely on generating outputs based on predefined context vectors or representations.

- Function: These models do not have an encoder; instead, they receive context vectors directly as input and generate corresponding outputs.

  - Example Application: Language generation tasks where the context vectors might represent prompts or initial conditions for generating text.

3. Full Encoder-Decoder Models:

  - Definition: Full encoder-decoder models include both encoder and decoder components, as described earlier.

  - Function: These models are used for tasks where input data needs to be transformed into meaningful output sequences or structures. They are particularly useful for tasks like machine translation, where the model needs to understand and generate sequences of different lengths and complexities.

  - Example Application: Neural machine translation systems where the encoder processes a source sentence and the decoder generates a translated sentence in the target language.

Applications and Advancements

The encoder-decoder architecture has revolutionized many fields within artificial intelligence and machine learning. Its flexibility and effectiveness have led to advancements in several areas:

- Machine Translation: Systems like Google Translate use encoder-decoder architectures to translate text between different languages.

- Image Captioning: Models can describe the content of images using natural language, enabled by encoder-decoder frameworks.

- Speech Recognition: Transcription systems convert spoken language into text, leveraging encoder-decoder structures for accuracy.

The encoder-decoder architecture represents a foundational framework in deep learning, enabling complex tasks such as translation, captioning, and speech recognition. By understanding the roles of the encoder and decoder components, as well as the variations in their configurations, researchers and practitioners can leverage this architecture to develop innovative solutions across various domains. As technology continues to evolve, encoder-decoder models are expected to remain at the forefront of advancements in artificial intelligence and machine learning.

This chapter has provided a comprehensive overview of the encoder-decoder architecture, from its structural components to its practical applications, highlighting its significance in contemporary deep learning research and development.

Chapter 10 Positional Encoding

Positional encoding is a crucial component in the architecture of transformers, which have revolutionized natural language processing (NLP) and other sequential data tasks. Transformers, first introduced in the seminal paper "Attention is All You Need" by Vaswani et al. in 2017, are adept at handling sequential data due to their self-attention mechanism. Unlike traditional recurrent neural networks (RNNs) or convolutional neural networks (CNNs), transformers do not inherently maintain sequence order in their architecture. Instead, they rely on positional encoding to provide information about the order of tokens in the input sequence. This essay explores how transformers handle sequential data, the different methods of positional encoding, and their implications for model performance.

How Transformers Handle Sequential Data

Transformers process sequential data by employing a mechanism known as self-attention. Self-attention allows the model to weigh the importance of each token in the sequence relative to every other token, capturing dependencies across different positions in the input. This ability to attend to different parts of the input sequence simultaneously is what gives transformers their advantage over traditional architectures in tasks like language modeling, translation, and text generation.

However, unlike RNNs which inherently encode sequential information due to their recurrent nature, transformers treat tokens independently of their position in the sequence by default. This lack of sequential order information could potentially limit the model's ability to understand sequences where the order of tokens matters (such as natural language sentences).

To address this limitation, transformers incorporate positional encoding. Positional encoding is a way to inject information about the position of tokens in the input sequence into the model. By adding positional encoding to the input embeddings, transformers enable the model to distinguish between tokens based not only on their content but also on their position in the sequence.

Different Methods of Positional Encoding

1. Sine and Cosine Positional Encodings

One of the most commonly used methods of positional encoding is based on sine and cosine functions. This method was introduced in the original transformer paper by Vaswani et al. The positional encoding for a token at position \(i \) and dimension \(j \) is calculated using the following formulas:

$$PE_{(i,2j)} = \sin\left(\frac{i}{10000^{2j/d_{\text{model}}}}\right)$$
$$PE_{(i,2j+1)} = \cos\left(\frac{i}{10000^{2j/d_{\text{model}}}}\right)$$

where \(i \) is the position of the token and \(j \) is the dimension of the positional encoding. \(d_{\text{model}} \) \) is the dimensionality of the model. These sine and cosine functions create a unique pattern for each position, allowing the model to learn the order of tokens within the sequence.

2. Learned Positional Encodings

Another approach is to learn positional embeddings along with the rest of the model parameters. In this method, instead of using fixed sinusoidal functions, the positional encodings are learned during the training process. This allows the model to adaptively adjust the positional information according to the task and the input data.

3. Absolute vs. Relative Positional Encodings

Absolute positional encodings, such as the sine and cosine positional encodings, encode the absolute position of each token in the sequence. On the other hand, relative positional encodings capture the relative distances or offsets between tokens. Relative positional encodings have been explored in recent research to improve the handling of long-range dependencies in transformers.

4. Hybrid and Contextual Positional Encodings

Hybrid approaches combine different positional encoding strategies to leverage their respective strengths. For example, some models use a combination of learned and sinusoidal positional encodings to benefit from both fixed patterns and adaptive adjustments. Contextual positional encodings vary the positional information based on the context of the sequence, allowing the model to focus more on relevant positions depending on the input.

Implications for Model Performance

The choice of positional encoding can significantly impact the performance of transformer models in various tasks. The effectiveness of positional encoding methods depends on the characteristics of the dataset, the length of sequences, and the complexity of the task.

- Long Sequences: Transformers with effective positional

encoding mechanisms can handle longer sequences compared to models without positional information, as they can maintain the order of tokens over greater distances.

- Generalization: Proper positional encoding helps transformers generalize better to unseen sequences by providing consistent positional information across different inputs.

- Task-specific Adaptation: The choice between fixed sinusoidal encoding and learned positional encoding often depends on whether the task requires a consistent representation of positional information or benefits from adaptive adjustments based on the input data.

Positional encoding plays a critical role in enabling transformers to effectively handle sequential data. By incorporating information about the position of tokens within the sequence, positional encoding allows transformers to surpass traditional models in tasks requiring understanding of sequential order, such as language modeling and translation. The evolution and refinement of positional encoding methods continue to be an active area of research, aiming to enhance the performance and applicability of transformers across various domains.

Chapter 11 Data Collection and Preprocessing

In the era of information abundance, data collection and preprocessing stand as crucial gateways to extracting meaningful insights and making informed decisions. This article explores the intricacies of sourcing and curating massive datasets, along with the essential techniques of text preprocessing.

Sourcing and Curating Massive Datasets

The advent of digital technologies has exponentially increased the volume and variety of data available for analysis. From social media interactions to sensor data in IoT devices, the sources of data are diverse and expansive. Sourcing these datasets involves several key steps:

Identifying Data Sources: Organizations must first identify relevant sources that align with their objectives. This could include internal databases, public repositories, APIs, or data purchased from third-party providers.

Data Collection Methods: Depending on the source, data collection methods vary widely. Web scraping, for instance, extracts data from websites, while APIs provide structured access to platforms like Twitter or Google Analytics. IoT devices continuously generate streams of sensor data that require real-time processing.

Legal and Ethical Considerations: With the increasing focus on data privacy and ethical concerns, organizations must navigate legal frameworks such as GDPR (General Data Protection Regulation) or CCPA (California Consumer Privacy Act). Compliance ensures that data collection practices respect user rights and privacy.

Data Quality Assurance: Ensuring data quality is paramount. Techniques such as data validation, cleaning, and normalization help maintain accuracy and consistency. Addressing issues like missing values or outliers early in the process prevents downstream analysis errors.

Data Integration: Often, data comes from disparate sources and in varying formats. Data integration involves harmonizing these sources into a unified format suitable for analysis. This step may include schema mapping, data transformation, and ensuring referential integrity.

Scalability and Storage: As datasets grow larger, scalability becomes critical. Cloud-based solutions offer scalable storage and computing resources, facilitating the handling of massive datasets without significant upfront infrastructure investment.

Text Preprocessing Techniques

Text data, whether from social media, customer reviews, or news articles, requires preprocessing to convert raw text into a format suitable for analysis and machine learning models.

Common techniques include:

Tokenization: Breaking text into smaller units such as words or n-grams. This step facilitates further analysis by converting the text into manageable units.

Lowercasing: Converting all text to lowercase standardizes words regardless of their original casing, reducing complexity and ensuring consistency.

Removing Noise: Noise includes irrelevant characters, punctuation, special characters, and HTML tags (in web data). Removing these enhances the quality and focus of the text analysis.

Stopword Removal: Stopwords are common words (e.g., "and", "the", "is") that add little semantic value. Removing stopwords reduces dimensionality and improves the focus on meaningful words.

Normalization: Techniques like stemming and lemmatization reduce words to their base or root form (e.g., "running" to "run"), reducing variant forms of words to a common base.

Handling Rare Words: Rare or infrequent words may be removed or replaced to prevent them from disproportionately influencing analysis results.

Feature Extraction: Transforming text into numerical representations (e.g., TF-IDF, word embeddings like Word2Vec or GloVe) enables machine learning algorithms to process and derive insights from text data.

Text Vectorization: Converting processed text into numerical vectors suitable for machine learning models. Techniques like Bag-of-Words (BoW) or Term Frequency-Inverse Document

Frequency (TF-IDF) are common approaches.

Data collection and preprocessing are foundational stages in the data analysis pipeline, crucial for deriving meaningful insights and making informed decisions. Sourcing and curating massive datasets involve navigating a landscape of diverse sources while adhering to legal and ethical standards. Text preprocessing techniques transform raw text into structured data, enabling powerful analyses and machine learning applications. As organizations continue to harness the power of data, mastering these processes becomes essential for unlocking the full potential of data-driven insights.

Chapter 12 Training Objectives

In Natural Language Processing (NLP), where machines learn to understand and generate human language, training objectives play a pivotal role. These objectives define the goals and metrics that guide algorithms in mastering linguistic tasks, such as masked language modeling and next-word prediction. Moreover, the significance of loss functions cannot be overstated; they act as the compass guiding the learning process, ensuring models iteratively improve their understanding and generation of language.

Understanding Masked Language Modeling

Masked language modeling is a technique where certain words in a sentence are masked or hidden, and the model is tasked with predicting what these masked words should be based on the context provided by the surrounding words. This objective is fundamental in training models to grasp syntactic and semantic nuances of language. Imagine teaching someone to fill in the blanks in a conversation where parts of the dialogue are intentionally obscured. The goal is to ensure that the learner comprehends the context well enough to accurately infer missing words, thereby enhancing their overall understanding of the conversation.

For a machine learning model, this translates into optimizing parameters to minimize the prediction error when filling in these blanks. The objective is not merely to memorize but to generalize from the patterns observed in the training data. Just as humans learn from exposure to diverse conversations, models trained on masked language modeling learn to predict missing words effectively across various contexts.

Next-Word Prediction: Anticipating Language Flow

Next-word prediction focuses on predicting the most likely word that follows a given sequence of words in a sentence or text. This task is akin to anticipating what comes next in a conversation based on the current topic and context. In human terms, it's like finishing someone's sentence accurately based on their previous statements and the ongoing discussion. This objective trains models to understand the flow of language, capturing both grammatical structures and semantic coherence.

The crux of next-word prediction lies in its application across different domains and styles of language. Just as humans adapt their predictions based on formal versus informal speech or specialized jargon, NLP models must discern and adapt to varying linguistic contexts. The training objective here is to refine the model's ability to probabilistically estimate the likelihood of each possible word following a given context, thereby improving the fluidity and naturalness of generated text.

Importance of Loss Functions

In machine learning, loss functions serve as the North Star guiding the optimization process. These functions quantify how well the model's predictions match the actual target values during training. For masked language modeling and next-word prediction, loss functions measure the discrepancy between predicted and actual words, steering the model towards minimizing errors and improving accuracy.

To humanize this concept, consider a teacher grading a student's homework. The teacher's objective is to minimize the difference between the expected answers (correct solutions) and the student's responses. Similarly, in NLP, loss functions evaluate how close the model's predictions are to the correct answers (words) in the training data. This iterative feedback loop ensures that the model adjusts its internal parameters to better capture the underlying patterns in language, ultimately enhancing its predictive capabilities. Loss functions also play a crucial role in balancing different aspects of model performance. For instance, in next-word prediction, a loss function might prioritize preserving grammatical correctness while also encouraging diversity in predicted outputs. This nuanced approach mirrors how humans balance clarity and creativity in their language use.

Humanizing the Training Process

Beyond technical metrics, the essence of training objectives lies in their broader implications for human-computer interaction and communication. By refining masked language modeling and next-word prediction, NLP models become more adept at understanding and generating human-like text. This proficiency is pivotal in applications ranging from chatbots that engage in natural conversations to language translation tools that preserve the nuances of expression across different languages and cultures.

The humanization of training objectives extends to the ethical considerations inherent in NLP advancements. As models become more proficient in understanding and generating language, it becomes imperative to ensure they do so responsibly and ethically. This involves addressing biases in training data, promoting inclusivity in language generation, and fostering transparency in how these models operate.

Training objectives such as masked language modeling and next-word prediction epitomize the journey towards enhancing NLP models' understanding and generation of human language. The importance of loss functions in this journey cannot be overlooked, as they provide the critical feedback necessary for models to refine their predictive accuracy. Ultimately, by humanizing these technical concepts, we underscore their transformative potential in shaping the future of communication and interaction between humans and machines.

Chapter 13 Optimization Algorithms

Optimization algorithms are at the heart of machine learning, driving the process of adjusting model parameters to minimize the error function. Among these, gradient descent, Adam, and other techniques play crucial roles. Additionally, fine-tuning hyperparameters is essential for achieving optimal model performance. This piece will delve into these optimization methods and explore the nuances of hyperparameter tuning.

Gradient descent is one of the most fundamental optimization algorithms used in machine learning. It aims to minimize a cost function $J(\theta)$ by iteratively moving towards the minimum point in the direction of the steepest descent.

Basic Concept

The cost function $J(\theta)$ is typically a measure of how far off a model's predictions are from the actual outcomes. The gradient of $J(\theta)$, denoted as $\nabla J(\theta)$, represents the direction and rate of the fastest increase of the function. Gradient descent updates the model parameters θ as follows:

$$\theta := \theta - \alpha \nabla J(\theta)$$

Gradient Descent

Gradient descent is one of the most fundamental optimization algorithms used in machine learning. It aims to minimize a cost function \(J(\theta) \) by iteratively moving towards the minimum point in the direction of the steepest descent.

Basic Concept

Variants of Gradient Descent

1. Batch Gradient Descent (BGD): This variant computes the gradient using the entire training dataset. While it provides a stable and accurate direction for the descent, it can be computationally expensive and slow for large datasets.

2. Stochastic Gradient Descent (SGD): Instead of using the whole dataset, SGD updates the parameters using one training example at a time. This introduces noise into the optimization process, which can help escape local minima but may lead to convergence issues.

3. Mini-batch Gradient Descent: This approach strikes a balance between BGD and SGD by updating the parameters based on a small random subset of the training data. It combines the computational efficiency of SGD with the stability of BGD.

Adam (Adaptive Moment Estimation)

Adam is an advanced optimization algorithm that combines the benefits of two other extensions of gradient descent: AdaGrad and RMSProp. It computes adaptive learning rates for each parameter.

Key Features

- Adaptive Learning Rates: Adam adjusts the learning rates for each parameter individually. This is done by maintaining two moving averages: the first moment (mean) and the second moment (uncentered variance) of the gradients.
- Bias Correction: Adam includes bias correction terms to account for the fact that the moving averages are initialized at zero and hence biased towards zero in the initial iterations. The parameter update rule for Adam is as follows:

$$m_t = \beta_1 m_{t-1} + (1 - \beta_1)g_t$$
$$v_t = \beta_2 v_{t-1} + (1 - \beta_2)g_t^2$$
$$\hat{m}_t = \frac{m_t}{1 - \beta_1^t}$$
$$\hat{v}_t = \frac{v_t}{1 - \beta_2^t}$$
$$\theta := \theta - \alpha \frac{\hat{m}_t}{\sqrt{\hat{v}_t} + \epsilon}$$

Here, g_t is the gradient at step t, m_t and v_t are the first and second moment estimates, β_1 and β_2 are the decay rates for these moments, and ϵ is a small constant to prevent division by zero.

Advantages

- Efficiency: Adam is computationally efficient and well-suited for large datasets or high-dimensional parameter spaces.

- Robustness: It requires less tuning of the learning rate and performs well with sparse gradients.

Other Optimization Techniques

Several other optimization algorithms are commonly used in machine learning, each with unique characteristics and use cases.

RMSProp (Root Mean quare Propagation)

RMSProp addresses some of the issues with AdaGrad by
introducing a moving average of squared gradients, which
helps in maintaining a more consistent learning rate.

$$v_t = \beta v_{t-1} + (1-\beta)g_t^2$$
$$\theta := \theta - \alpha \frac{g_t}{\sqrt{v_t}+\epsilon}$$

RMSProp is particularly useful for training deep neural networks.

AdaGrad (Adaptive Gradient Algorithm)

AdaGrad adapts the learning rate for each parameter based on the past gradients. Parameters with
large gradients get smaller updates, and those with small gradients get larger updates.

$$\theta := \theta - \alpha \frac{g_t}{\sqrt{G_t}+\epsilon}$$

Here, G_t is a diagonal matrix where each element G_{ii} is the sum of the squares of the gradients up
to time t.

Fine-tuning Hyperparameters

Hyperparameters are the parameters set before the learning

process begins and are not updated during training. Fine-tuning these hyperparameters is critical for the performance of machine learning models.

Common Hyperparameters

1. Learning Rate: Controls how much to change the model in response to the estimated error each time the model weights are updated.

2. Batch Size: Number of training examples utilized in one iteration.

3. Number of Epochs: Number of complete passes through the training dataset.

4. Regularization Parameters: Parameters such as L2 regularization strength to prevent overfitting.

5. Dropout Rate: Used in neural networks to prevent overfitting by randomly setting a fraction of input units to

zero at each update during training time.

Hyperparameter Tuning Techniques

1. Grid Search: Exhaustive searching through a manually specified subset of the hyperparameter space. It is simple but can be computationally expensive.

2. Random Search: Samples hyperparameters randomly instead of exhaustively searching all possible combinations. It often finds good hyperparameters more quickly than grid search.

3. Bayesian Optimization: Uses probabilistic models to find the optimal hyperparameters. It is more efficient than grid and random search as it uses prior results to choose the next set of hyperparameters to evaluate.

4. Hyperband: An efficient algorithm for hyperparameter optimization that combines random search with early

stopping. It allocates more resources to promising configurations and discards poor performers early.

5. Genetic Algorithms: Inspired by natural selection, these algorithms evolve a population of hyperparameter sets over several generations. They use operations like mutation and crossover to explore the hyperparameter space.

Practical Considerations

Initial Learning Rate

Choosing an appropriate initial learning rate is crucial. If the learning rate is too high, the algorithm might overshoot the minimum. If it's too low, the convergence will be slow. A learning rate schedule, where the learning rate decreases over time, can help in achieving better results.

Batch Size

The choice of batch size affects the speed and stability of the training process. Smaller batch sizes provide a regularizing effect and lead to faster convergence, but they introduce more noise into the gradient estimation. Larger batch sizes offer a more accurate gradient estimation but can lead to slower convergence.

Number of Epochs

The number of epochs should be chosen based on the specific problem and dataset. Too few epochs can lead to underfitting, while too many can lead to overfitting. Early stopping is a useful technique to terminate training when performance on a validation set starts to degrade.

Regularization

Regularization techniques like L2 regularization, dropout, and batch normalization help in preventing overfitting by adding constraints to the model. These techniques should be carefully tuned to balance model complexity and generalization.

Learning Rate Schedulers

Using learning rate schedulers, which adjust the learning rate during training, can significantly improve performance. Common schedulers include step decay, exponential decay, and adaptive learning rates (as used in Adam).

Optimization algorithms and hyperparameter tuning are critical components of machine learning. Gradient descent and its variants, along with advanced optimizers like Adam, provide powerful tools for model training. Fine-tuning hyperparameters through various techniques can significantly impact model performance. By understanding and leveraging these methods, practitioners can develop more accurate and robust machine learning models.

Chapter 14 Scaling Up

The evolution from GPT-2 to GPT-4 marks a significant milestone in the development of natural language processing (NLP) models. This progression showcases not only the advancements in model architecture and capabilities but also the increasing complexity and computational demands involved in training and deploying these models. This essay will explore the key aspects of this transition, focusing on the implications of increasing model size and the computational challenges encountered along with the solutions devised to address them.

Increasing Model Size and Its Implications

The journey from GPT-2 to GPT-4 involved a substantial increase in model size, characterized by the number of parameters. GPT-2, released by OpenAI in 2019, featured 1.5 billion parameters, a significant leap from its predecessor, GPT. This expansion enabled GPT-2 to generate more coherent and contextually relevant text, demonstrating a marked improvement in language understanding and generation.

However, GPT-3, which followed in 2020, took an even more dramatic leap, boasting 175 billion parameters. This exponential increase in model size brought several implications:

Enhanced Capabilities: The massive scale of GPT-3 allowed it to perform a wide range of tasks with little to no fine-tuning, a phenomenon known as few-shot learning. This meant that the model could understand and generate human-like text across various contexts, making it versatile and powerful.

Improved Contextual Understanding: Larger models can better capture long-range dependencies in text, which improves their ability to maintain context over extended passages. This is crucial for generating coherent and contextually accurate text in applications like conversational agents and content creation.

Resource Intensiveness: The increase in model size also brought significant computational and resource challenges. Training and running inference on such a large model require immense computational power, memory, and storage, making it more expensive and less accessible for smaller organizations and researchers.

Ethical and Social Implications: The ability of large models to generate highly realistic text also raised concerns about misinformation, deepfakes, and the potential for misuse in various domains. Ensuring responsible and ethical use of these powerful tools became a critical focus.

With GPT-4, the trend of scaling up continued, although specific details about the number of parameters were not disclosed at the time of its release. Nonetheless, it is widely understood that GPT-4 represents an improvement over GPT-3 in terms of both size and sophistication.

Computational Challenges and Solutions

Scaling up NLP models from GPT-2 to GPT-4 involved numerous computational challenges. Addressing these challenges required innovative solutions in hardware, software, and algorithmic design.

Hardware Limitations: The sheer scale of models like GPT-3

and GPT-4 demands advanced hardware. Traditional CPUs are insufficient for the parallel processing required to train these models. Instead, GPUs and TPUs (Tensor Processing Units) are used, providing the necessary computational power and efficiency.

 - Solution: Companies like NVIDIA and Google have developed specialized hardware optimized for deep learning tasks. NVIDIA's A100 GPUs and Google's TPU v4 are examples of cutting-edge technology designed to handle the computational load of training large-scale models.

Memory Management: Training models with billions of parameters requires extensive memory management. The memory bandwidth and capacity of GPUs and TPUs are critical constraints.

 - Solution: Techniques such as model parallelism and

pipeline parallelism have been employed. Model parallelism involves splitting the model across multiple devices, while pipeline parallelism divides the computation into stages that can be processed concurrently. Additionally, mixed precision training, which uses lower-precision arithmetic, reduces memory usage without significantly affecting performance.

Data and Storage: The training process for models like GPT-3 and GPT-4 requires vast amounts of data, which must be stored and efficiently accessed.

- Solution: Distributed storage systems and data sharding are used to manage and access large datasets. These systems split the data across multiple storage devices, enabling faster data retrieval and processing.

Training Time and Cost: Training a model like GPT-3 can

take weeks and cost millions of dollars. Optimizing the training process to reduce time and cost is a major challenge.

- Solution: Efficient optimization algorithms and techniques such as gradient accumulation, large batch sizes, and distributed training are employed to speed up the training process. Moreover, companies are increasingly using cloud-based infrastructures, which offer scalable resources on-demand, helping to manage costs more effectively.

Scalability: Ensuring that the training infrastructure can scale to accommodate the growing size of models is critical.

- Solution: Scalable architecture designs, such as those offered by cloud service providers (e.g., AWS, Azure, Google Cloud), allow researchers to dynamically allocate resources based on the needs of the model. These platforms offer tools and services specifically designed for distributed computing and large-scale machine learning.

 Algorithmic Innovations: Scaling up models is not just about adding more parameters; it also involves improving the underlying algorithms to make them more efficient and effective.

 - Solution: Techniques such as sparse attention, which focuses on the most relevant parts of the input, can reduce computational complexity. Additionally, innovations in model architecture, such as the use of transformers, have played a significant role in managing the increased complexity of larger models.

Future Directions

The transition from GPT-2 to GPT-4 highlights both the

progress and the ongoing challenges in the field of NLP. As we look to the future, several trends and areas of research are likely to shape the continued evolution of large language models: Efficiency and Sustainability: Given the significant computational resources required for training large models, there is a growing emphasis on developing more efficient and sustainable AI.

This includes research into energy-efficient algorithms, reducing the carbon footprint of training, and exploring alternative computing paradigms such as quantum computing.

Fine-Tuning and Adaptation: While few-shot learning is a powerful capability, there is still a need for models that can be easily fine-tuned and adapted to specific tasks and domains with minimal data. Techniques such as transfer learning and continual learning are likely to become increasingly important.

Multimodal Models: The integration of multiple types of data (e.g., text, images, audio) into a single model represents a significant frontier in AI research. Multimodal models can enhance understanding and generation capabilities, leading to more versatile and intelligent systems.

Ethical AI and Governance: As models become more powerful, the need for robust ethical guidelines and governance frameworks becomes more critical. Ensuring that AI is developed and deployed responsibly, with considerations for bias, fairness, and transparency, is essential.

Accessibility and Democratization: Making advanced AI technologies accessible to a broader range of users, including smaller organizations and individual researchers, is an important goal.

This involves developing more user-friendly tools and

platforms, as well as open-sourcing models and datasets where appropriate.

The evolution from GPT-2 to GPT-4 exemplifies the rapid advancements and increasing complexity in the field of natural language processing. The implications of scaling up model size are profound, offering enhanced capabilities and improved contextual understanding while also introducing significant computational and ethical challenges. Addressing these challenges has required innovative solutions in hardware, software, and algorithmic design, pushing the boundaries of what is possible in AI.

As we continue to develop even more sophisticated models, the focus will likely shift towards making AI more efficient, sustainable, and accessible, while ensuring ethical considerations remain at the forefront.

The journey from GPT-2 to GPT-4 is just one step in the ongoing quest to create more intelligent and versatile AI systems, promising a future where machines can understand and generate human language with unprecedented accuracy and nuance.

Chapter 15 Fine-Tuning Techniques

Fine-tuning techniques in machine learning, especially within the realm of deep learning, play a pivotal role in adapting pretrained models to specific tasks. This approach not only saves computational resources but also leverages the knowledge gained from large datasets during pretraining. In this essay, we delve into various methods of fine-tuning models, explore the advantages of transfer learning, and discuss its broader implications in the field of artificial intelligence.

Fine-tuning refers to the process of taking a pretrained model and adapting it to a new, specific task by further training it on task-specific data. This method is particularly effective in scenarios where the target task shares similarities with the tasks the model was originally trained on. The underlying principle is to adjust the weights of the pretrained model's layers to better fit the nuances and requirements of the new task.

Methods for Fine-Tuning on Specific Tasks

Feature Extraction and Fine-Tuning:

- In feature extraction, the early layers of a pretrained model, such as convolutional layers in CNNs trained on ImageNet, are used as feature extractors. These features are then fed into a new classifier specific to the target task. This method is efficient when the dataset for the target task is small or when computational resources are limited.

- Fine-tuning involves updating the weights of the entire

pretrained model, typically using a smaller learning rate to avoid losing the general knowledge captured during pretraining. This approach is more suitable when the target task dataset is large and diverse enough to warrant adjusting the entire model.

Layer-specific Fine-Tuning

- Depending on the task, specific layers of the pretrained model may be fine-tuned while freezing others. For instance, in natural language processing tasks, the lower layers of a Transformer model like BERT might be frozen to retain general linguistic knowledge, while higher layers are fine-tuned to adapt to domain-specific nuances.

Domain-Specific Fine-Tuning

- Sometimes, fine-tuning involves not just adjusting model parameters but also modifying the architecture or preprocessing steps to better align with the target domain's characteristics. For example, in medical imaging, pretrained models might be fine-tuned with additional data augmentation techniques specific to medical images to enhance performance and generalization.

Iterative Fine-Tuning:

- Iterative fine-tuning involves multiple rounds of fine-tuning on progressively more specific datasets or tasks. This iterative approach allows the model to gradually adapt to finer details of the target task, thereby improving performance incrementally.

Transfer Learning and Its Benefits

Transfer learning forms the foundation of fine-tuning techniques, enabling models to transfer knowledge learned from one domain or task to another. The benefits of transfer learning are manifold and include:

Reduced Training Time and Resource Requirements:

   - By leveraging pretrained models, transfer learning reduces the computational resources and time required to achieve good performance on new tasks. This is especially advantageous in scenarios where training from scratch would be impractical due to data or resource constraints.

Improved Generalization:

   - Pretrained models, having learned representations from large and diverse datasets, capture general features of the data domain. Fine-tuning these models on task-specific data helps in adapting these general features to the nuances of the new task, thereby improving generalization on unseen data.

Effective Feature Extraction:

- In tasks where labeled data is scarce, feature extraction from pretrained models provides a powerful method for obtaining meaningful representations of input data. These representations can then be used as input to simpler classifiers or models, leading to improved performance.

Continuous Learning and Adaptation:

- Transfer learning facilitates continuous learning and adaptation in dynamic environments. As new data becomes available or tasks evolve, pretrained models can be updated or fine-tuned without starting from scratch, ensuring models remain relevant and effective over time.

Domain-Specific Knowledge Transfer:

- Pretrained models often encode domain-specific knowledge learned from vast datasets. By fine-tuning these models on related tasks within the same domain, such as medical imaging or natural language processing, valuable domain-specific insights are transferred, leading to enhanced performance.

Applications and Future Directions

The application of fine-tuning techniques and transfer learning extends across various domains:

- Computer Vision: In image classification, object detection, and segmentation tasks, models like ResNet, VGG, and EfficientNet pretrained on ImageNet are commonly fine-tuned to achieve state-of-the-art results on specific datasets such as COCO or CIFAR.

- Natural Language Processing: Transformers like BERT, GPT, and their variants pretrained on large text corpora are fine-tuned for tasks such as sentiment analysis, question answering, and text generation. This approach significantly improves performance, particularly in tasks where labeled data is limited.

- Healthcare: Fine-tuning pretrained models on medical imaging data enhances diagnostic accuracy and aids in disease detection. Models pretrained on general datasets can be adapted to identify specific abnormalities or diseases with high sensitivity and specificity.

Looking forward, ongoing research focuses on improving transfer learning techniques to handle even more diverse tasks and domains. Techniques like self-supervised learning, where models learn from unlabeled data, promise to further enhance the capabilities of pretrained models by reducing reliance on labeled datasets.

Fine-tuning techniques and transfer learning have revolutionized the field of machine learning by allowing pretrained models to adapt to specific tasks efficiently. By leveraging knowledge learned from large datasets, these techniques enable rapid development of high-performance models across various domains. As research progresses and computational capabilities advance, the synergy between transfer learning and fine-tuning promises to drive further innovation, making AI systems more adaptable, efficient, and capable of solving complex real-world problems.

Chapter 16 Task-Specific Adaptations

The natural language processing (NLP) has led to the development of versatile and sophisticated models capable of performing a variety of tasks. Among these tasks, translation, summarization, and question-answering (QA) stand out as particularly challenging and widely used applications. While large-scale pre-trained language models (e.g., GPT, BERT) provide a strong foundation, fine-tuning these models for specific tasks enhances their performance by tailoring their capabilities to the nuances of each task. This document explores the fine-tuning process for these tasks, illustrating the approach with case studies and examples.

Fine-Tuning for Translation

Translation is the process of converting text from one language to another. Fine-tuning for translation involves adapting a pre-trained language model to accurately map input text in the source language to output text in the target language. This process requires a large parallel corpus (i.e., text aligned sentence-by-sentence in both languages).

Case Study: Fine-Tuning BERT for English-French Translation

1. Data Preparation:

   - Parallel Corpus: The fine-tuning process starts with a parallel corpus, such as the WMT dataset, which contains sentence pairs in English and French.

   - Tokenization: Both English and French texts are

tokenized using a subword tokenization method (e.g., Byte Pair Encoding).

2. Model Adaptation:

- Model Selection: A pre-trained language model like mBERT (multilingual BERT) is chosen due to its multilingual capabilities.

- Architecture Adjustment: The model is adjusted to include an encoder-decoder architecture, where the encoder processes the English input, and the decoder generates the French output.

3. Training Process:

- Objective Function: The objective is to minimize the cross-entropy loss between the predicted and actual translations.

- Optimization: Techniques like learning rate scheduling

and gradient clipping are employed to stabilize training.

4. Evaluation:

  - Metrics: BLEU (Bilingual Evaluation Understudy) score is commonly used to evaluate the quality of translations.

  - Human Evaluation: A subset of translations may be evaluated by bilingual speakers to assess fluency and accuracy.

Example:

  - Input (English): "The quick brown fox jumps over the lazy dog."

  - Output (French): "Le renard brun rapide saute par-dessus le chien paresseux."

By fine-tuning mBERT with a parallel English-French corpus, the model learns the syntactic and semantic correspondences between the two languages, resulting in high-quality translations.

Fine-Tuning for Summarization

Summarization involves condensing a longer text into a shorter version while preserving the key information. There are two main types of summarization: extractive (selecting sentences directly from the text) and abstractive (generating new sentences that capture the essence of the text).

Case Study: Fine-Tuning GPT-3 for News Article Summarization

1. Data Preparation:

   - Dataset: A dataset like CNN/Daily Mail is used, which contains news articles paired with human-written summaries.

   - Preprocessing: Articles and summaries are preprocessed,

including tokenization and truncation to handle the input size limit.

2. Model Adaptation:

- Model Selection: GPT-3, with its powerful generative capabilities, is selected.

- Architecture: The transformer architecture of GPT-3 is inherently suitable for abstractive summarization due to its capacity to generate coherent and contextually relevant text.

3. Training Process:

- Fine-Tuning: The model is fine-tuned on the article-summary pairs, learning to generate summaries that capture the main points of the articles.

- Loss Function: The training optimizes the likelihood of the generated summary matching the reference summary.

4. Evaluation:

  - ROUGE Score: ROUGE (Recall-Oriented Understudy for Gisting Evaluation) measures overlap between the generated and reference summaries.

  - Quality Assessment: Human evaluation may be used to assess readability and informativeness.

Example:

  - Input (Article): A news article detailing a political event.

  - Output (Summary): "The government announced new policies to tackle economic challenges, aiming to boost growth and employment."

Through fine-tuning, GPT-3 learns to distill the essence of news articles into concise summaries that convey the most critical information, maintaining coherence and relevance.

Fine-Tuning for Question-Answering

Question-answering (QA) involves retrieving accurate answers to questions based on a given context. QA models can be either open-domain (answering questions from a vast range of topics) or closed-domain (focused on a specific area).

Case Study: Fine-Tuning BERT for SQuAD QA

1. Data Preparation:

   - Dataset: SQuAD (Stanford Question Answering Dataset) provides context paragraphs and corresponding questions with annotated answers.

   - Preprocessing: Text is tokenized, and context-question pairs are formatted for input into the model.

2. Model Adaptation:

   - Model Selection: BERT, known for its strong
performance in QA tasks, is chosen.

   - Architecture: BERT's architecture includes an embedding
layer, transformer blocks, and a prediction head for start and
end positions of the answer span.

3. Training Process:

   - Fine-Tuning: BERT is fine-tuned on the SQuAD dataset,
learning to predict the start and end tokens of the answer
span within the context.

   - Objective Function: The training optimizes for the correct
identification of the answer span in the context.

4. Evaluation:

   - Exact Match (EM): Measures the percentage of answers
that match the ground truth exactly.

   - F1 Score: Evaluates the overlap between predicted and
actual answers, balancing precision and recall.

Example:

- Input (Context): A paragraph about the solar system.

- Question: "What is the largest planet in our solar system?"

- Output (Answer): "Jupiter."

By fine-tuning BERT on the SQuAD dataset, the model learns to locate and extract precise answers from a given context, achieving high accuracy in QA tasks.

Fine-tuning pre-trained language models for specific tasks like translation, summarization, and question-answering significantly enhances their performance by aligning their capabilities with the requirements of each task. Through careful data preparation, model adaptation, and rigorous training and evaluation processes, these models can be adapted to deliver high-quality outputs tailored to the unique demands of each application.

Translation benefits from large parallel corpora and models capable of understanding multiple languages, such as mBERT. Summarization leverages the generative strengths of models like GPT-3 to produce coherent and concise summaries. Question-Answering exploits the contextual understanding of models like BERT to accurately pinpoint answers within a given text.

Each task-specific adaptation showcases the power of fine-tuning in creating specialized tools from versatile, pre-trained language models, ultimately pushing the boundaries of what NLP technologies can achieve.

Chapter 17 Text Generation Mechanisms

Text generation mechanisms have evolved significantly with the advent of large language models (LLMs) like GPT-4, BERT, and others. These models can generate coherent and contextually relevant text, largely due to sophisticated underlying architectures and advanced sampling techniques. In this document, we will explore how LLMs generate text, focusing on their architecture, training processes, and techniques like beam search and top-k sampling that enhance their text generation capabilities.

How LLMs Generate Coherent and Contextually Relevant
Text

1. Transformer Architecture

The foundation of most modern LLMs is the transformer
architecture, introduced by Vaswani et al. in 2017. Unlike
previous models that relied heavily on recurrent neural
networks (RNNs) or convolutional neural networks (CNNs),
transformers utilize self-attention mechanisms, enabling them
to process and generate text more effectively.

Self-Attention Mechanism

The self-attention mechanism allows the model to weigh the
importance of different words in a sentence relative to each

other. This is crucial for understanding context, as it helps the model consider the entire sequence of words rather than just the immediate neighbors, which is a limitation in RNNs.

In self-attention, the input sequence is transformed into three matrices: Query (Q), Key (K), and Value (V). The attention score for each word is calculated by taking the dot product of the Query with all Keys, followed by a softmax operation. This score is then used to weigh the Values, producing a weighted sum that represents the context-aware embedding of each word.

$$\text{Attention}(Q, K, V) = \text{softmax}\left(\frac{QK^T}{\sqrt{d_k}}\right) V$$

This mechanism is repeated across multiple layers, each layer refining the representation of the input text.

Positional Encoding

Transformers lack the sequential nature of RNNs, which means they do not inherently understand the order of words. To address this, positional encoding is added to the input embeddings, providing information about the position of each word in the sequence. These encodings are added to the input embeddings at the initial layer, allowing the model to capture word order and sentence structure.

2. Training on Large Datasets

LLMs are trained on vast datasets that cover a wide range of topics, languages, and contexts. The training process involves:

Pretraining

During pretraining, the model learns general language representations from large corpora. Tasks like masked language modeling (MLM) and next sentence prediction (NSP) are commonly used. In MLM, some words in the input are masked, and the model must predict them. NSP involves predicting whether two sentences follow each other in a document, helping the model understand sentence-level relationships.

Fine-Tuning

After pretraining, the model undergoes fine-tuning on specific tasks or datasets to specialize in particular areas. This step further refines the model's understanding and helps it generate more contextually relevant text for specific applications.

Techniques for Text Generation: Beam Search and Top-k Sampling

Generating text from an LLM involves predicting the next word in a sequence, which can be approached in several ways. Two prominent techniques are beam search and top-k sampling.

Beam Search

Beam search is a deterministic technique used to generate text sequences. It aims to find the most probable sequence of words by maintaining multiple hypotheses (beams) at each step.

How Beam Search Works

1. Initialization: Start with the initial token (e.g., <|endoftext|>) and initialize a list of beams with their corresponding probabilities.

2. Expansion: At each step, expand each beam by generating all possible next words along with their probabilities.

3. Pruning: From the expanded list, select the top B beams (where B is the beam width) based on their cumulative probabilities.

4. Iteration: Repeat the expansion and pruning steps until a stopping criterion is met (e.g., a predefined sequence length or an end-of-sequence token).

Advantages and Limitations

Beam search is effective in finding high-probability sequences and ensures that the generated text is coherent and grammatically correct. However, it has limitations:

- Computationally Intensive: Maintaining multiple beams requires significant computational resources.

- Diversity: It may generate repetitive or less diverse text because it prioritizes the most probable sequences.

Top-k Sampling

Top-k sampling is a probabilistic technique that introduces randomness into the text generation process, enhancing diversity.

How Top-k Sampling Works

1. Initialization: Start with the initial token and generate probabilities for all possible next words.
2. Filtering: Select the top k words with the highest probabilities.

3. Sampling: Randomly sample the next word from the top k words based on their probabilities.

4. Iteration: Repeat the process until a stopping criterion is met.

Advantages and Limitations

Top-k sampling balances coherence and diversity by allowing less probable words to be part of the generated text. This results in more creative and varied outputs. However, it can occasionally produce less coherent sequences if too much randomness is introduced.

Advanced Techniques

Top-p (Nucleus) Sampling

Top-p sampling (or nucleus sampling) is a variation of top-k sampling where the top-p words are selected based on their cumulative probability, ensuring that the total probability is above a certain threshold (p).

How Top-p Sampling Works

1. Initialization: Start with the initial token and generate probabilities for all possible next words.

2. Cumulative Filtering: Select words until their cumulative probability exceeds the threshold p.

3. Sampling: Randomly sample the next word from the selected set based on their probabilities.

4. Iteration: Repeat the process until a stopping criterion is met.

Top-p sampling dynamically adjusts the number of candidates

based on their probabilities, offering a balance between coherence and diversity similar to top-k sampling but with more flexibility.

Temperature Sampling

Temperature sampling controls the randomness of predictions by scaling the logits (the raw predictions) before applying the softmax function.

$$P(w_i) = \frac{\exp(\frac{logit(w_i)}{T})}{\sum_j \exp(\frac{logit(w_j)}{T})}$$

Where T is the temperature parameter:

- $T < 1$: Makes the model more confident and deterministic.
- $T > 1$: Increases randomness and diversity in the output.

Combining Techniques

Advanced text generation often combines these techniques to

achieve desired outcomes. For instance, beam search can be used for initial sequence generation followed by top-k or top-p sampling to inject diversity. Temperature scaling can be adjusted dynamically based on the context or the stage of generation.

Applications and Challenges

LLMs have numerous applications, including content creation, dialogue systems, code generation, and more. They are used in virtual assistants, automated writing tools, customer service bots, and even in creative writing and game development.

However, challenges remain:

- Bias and Fairness: LLMs can inadvertently learn and propagate biases present in training data.

- Ethical Considerations: The potential for misuse, such as

generating misleading information or deepfake texts, raises
ethical concerns.

- Resource Intensiveness: Training and deploying LLMs
require significant computational resources and energy,
impacting accessibility and sustainability.

Future Directions

The field of text generation continues to evolve, with ongoing
research focusing on improving model efficiency, reducing
biases, and enhancing contextual understanding. Future
directions include:

- Efficient Training Techniques: Developing methods to
reduce the computational requirements for training and fine-
tuning.

- Context-Aware Models: Enhancing models to better
understand and maintain long-term context across longer text

sequences.

- Robustness and Safety: Implementing mechanisms to detect and mitigate harmful or biased outputs.

Text generation mechanisms in LLMs, powered by the transformer architecture and advanced sampling techniques like beam search and top-k sampling, have revolutionized the field of natural language processing. These models can generate coherent, contextually relevant, and diverse text, making them invaluable in various applications. Despite the challenges, continuous advancements promise to make these models more efficient, fair, and ethically sound, paving the way for more sophisticated and responsible AI-driven text generation in the future.

Chapter 18 Controlling Output Quality

Controlling the quality of output is essential in various domains such as writing, artificial intelligence, manufacturing, and software development. This essay focuses on the methods to control output quality in the context of writing and artificial intelligence, emphasizing coherence, relevance, and creativity. These three aspects are critical for producing work that is not only technically correct but also engaging and meaningful for the intended audience.

Coherence

Coherence refers to the logical flow and connectivity of ideas in a piece of writing. It ensures that the output is easy to understand and follows a clear structure. Achieving coherence can be challenging, but several methods can help maintain it:

1. Outlining and Planning:

   - Pre-writing Outline: Creating an outline before starting the writing process helps in organizing thoughts and ensuring a logical progression of ideas. This outline serves as a roadmap, guiding the writer through the main points and supporting details.

   - Structured Planning: Breaking down the content into sections and subsections allows for a hierarchical structure where each part naturally flows into the next. This structured approach helps in maintaining coherence throughout the document.

2. Transitional Devices:

   - Transitional Words and Phrases: Using transitional words

and phrases like "however," "therefore," "furthermore," and "consequently" helps in linking sentences and paragraphs smoothly. These transitions act as bridges, connecting different parts of the text.

  - Thematic Consistency: Ensuring that each paragraph starts with a topic sentence that reflects the main idea helps in maintaining thematic consistency. Each paragraph should logically follow the previous one, contributing to the overall coherence.

3. Revising and Editing:

  - Multiple Revisions: Revising the content multiple times helps in identifying and correcting any incoherent parts. Each revision should focus on different aspects, such as overall structure, paragraph flow, and sentence clarity.

  - Peer Review: Having others review the content provides a fresh perspective. Peer reviewers can point out parts that are confusing or lack coherence, enabling the writer to make necessary adjustments.

4. Tools and Technologies:

  - Grammar and Style Checkers: Tools like Grammarly and Hemingway Editor help in identifying grammatical errors and improving sentence structure, which contributes to coherence.

  - AI Writing Assistants: Advanced AI tools like GPT-4 can provide suggestions for improving coherence by analyzing the text's flow and making recommendations.

Relevance

Relevance ensures that the content is pertinent to the topic and meets the needs and expectations of the audience. Controlling relevance involves several strategies:

1. Audience Analysis:

   - Understanding the Audience: Knowing the audience's preferences, knowledge level, and expectations helps in tailoring the content to be relevant. This involves researching the target audience and considering their needs.

   - Purpose Alignment: Clearly defining the purpose of the writing and aligning it with the audience's interests ensures relevance. The content should address the audience's questions, concerns, or interests directly.

2. Content Curation:

   - Selective Information: Including only information that is directly related to the topic prevents the inclusion of irrelevant details. This selective approach keeps the content focused and pertinent.

   - Fact-Checking: Ensuring that all facts and information are accurate and up-to-date maintains relevance. This involves rigorous research and verification of sources.

3. Iterative Feedback:

   - Continuous Feedback Loop: Regularly seeking feedback from the audience or peers helps in gauging relevance. Feedback can highlight areas that need more focus or those that are unnecessary.

   - Adaptive Writing: Being open to making changes based on feedback helps in keeping the content relevant. This adaptive approach ensures that the writing evolves to meet the audience's needs.

4. Use of Examples and Case Studies:

   - Real-World Examples: Incorporating examples and case studies relevant to the audience's experiences or interests makes the content more relatable and engaging.

- Contextualization: Placing information in the context of the audience's environment or experiences enhances relevance. This contextual approach helps in making the content more meaningful.

Creativity

Creativity involves presenting ideas in a novel and engaging manner. It is essential for capturing the audience's attention and making the content stand out. Methods to enhance creativity include:

1. Brainstorming and Ideation:
   - Divergent Thinking: Encouraging divergent thinking, where multiple ideas are generated without immediate judgment, fosters creativity. This brainstorming process allows for the exploration of unconventional ideas.

- Mind Mapping: Creating mind maps to visually organize ideas helps in seeing connections and generating new concepts. This visual approach can inspire creative solutions and narratives.

2. Incorporating Different Perspectives:

   - Multidisciplinary Approach: Drawing inspiration from different fields and disciplines can lead to unique ideas. This cross-pollination of ideas enhances creativity by introducing new perspectives.

   - Collaborative Creativity: Working with others, especially from diverse backgrounds, can spark creative ideas. Collaboration encourages the exchange of ideas and fosters a creative environment.

3. Experimentation and Playfulness:

   - Free Writing: Engaging in free writing exercises, where

ideas are written down without concern for structure or correctness, can unleash creativity. This playful approach helps in overcoming writer's block and generating fresh ideas.

- Creative Constraints: Imposing creative constraints, such as writing within a specific word limit or using a particular narrative style, can stimulate creative thinking. Constraints challenge the writer to think outside the box.

4. Use of Analogies and Metaphors:

- Analogical Thinking: Using analogies and metaphors to explain complex ideas in simpler terms can enhance creativity. Analogical thinking helps in making connections between seemingly unrelated concepts.

- Metaphorical Language: Employing metaphorical language adds depth and creativity to the writing. Metaphors can make abstract ideas more tangible and engaging.

5. Inspiration from Art and Literature:

  - Reading Widely: Exposure to different genres of literature and forms of art can inspire creative ideas. Reading widely helps in understanding various narrative techniques and styles.

  - Artistic Techniques: Applying artistic techniques, such as storytelling, vivid imagery, and symbolism, enhances the creative quality of writing. These techniques make the content more appealing and memorable.

Implementing Methods in AI Writing

In the context of artificial intelligence, particularly with models like GPT-4, controlling output quality involves programming and algorithmic strategies to ensure coherence, relevance, and creativity. Here's how these methods are implemented:

1. Algorithmic Coherence:

- Sequential Modelling: Using advanced sequential models like transformers ensures that the AI understands and maintains the context throughout the text. These models are trained to predict the next word based on the previous ones, maintaining coherence.

- Context Windows: Implementing large context windows allows the AI to consider a broader context, ensuring that the output remains coherent over longer passages.

2. Relevance through Training Data:

- Curated Training Data: Training AI models on curated datasets that reflect relevant and high-quality information ensures that the generated content is pertinent. This involves filtering out irrelevant or low-quality data during the training phase.

- Fine-Tuning: Fine-tuning models on specific domains or

topics helps in generating more relevant content. This specialized training ensures that the AI understands the nuances of the subject matter.

3. Creativity via Generative Techniques:

  - Creative Algorithms: Implementing algorithms that encourage creativity, such as those using reinforcement learning, helps in generating novel ideas. These algorithms reward the AI for producing unique and engaging content.

  - Prompt Engineering: Using creative prompts and seed texts can guide the AI to generate more creative outputs. Prompt engineering involves designing prompts that inspire creative responses from the model.

4. Feedback and Iteration:

  - Human-in-the-Loop: Incorporating human feedback in

the training and refinement process ensures that the AI's outputs are continually improved. Human reviewers can provide insights into coherence, relevance, and creativity, which are then used to adjust the model.

- Adaptive Learning: Implementing adaptive learning techniques allows the AI to learn from new data and feedback, ensuring that it remains relevant and capable of generating creative content.

Controlling output quality in writing and artificial intelligence involves a multifaceted approach that addresses coherence, relevance, and creativity. For human writers, this includes structured planning, iterative feedback, and creative thinking techniques.

In the realm of AI, it involves sophisticated algorithms, curated training data, and continuous feedback mechanisms. By implementing these methods, both human and AI writers can produce high-quality, engaging, and meaningful content

that meets the needs and expectations of their audience.

Chapter 19 Handling Ambiguity and Context

Handling ambiguity and maintaining context over long text generation are critical components in developing sophisticated natural language processing (NLP) systems, such as conversational agents, chatbots, and text generators. These systems must navigate the challenges posed by ambiguous language and the complexity of maintaining context to provide coherent, relevant, and accurate responses. This document explores strategies to maintain context over long text generation and address ambiguity in user inputs.

Strategies to Maintain Context Over Long Text Generation

Maintaining context in long text generation involves ensuring that the generated text remains coherent and relevant to the ongoing discussion or narrative. Here are some effective strategies to achieve this:

1. Hierarchical Attention Mechanisms

Hierarchical attention mechanisms allow models to focus on different levels of context, such as sentence-level and document-level context. By hierarchically structuring the attention, the model can dynamically select and emphasize the most relevant parts of the input text, thus maintaining a coherent narrative or response over long text generations.

2. Memory-Augmented Neural Networks

Memory-augmented neural networks, like the Neural Turing Machine or Differentiable Neural Computer, enhance traditional neural networks with external memory components. These memory structures enable the model to store and retrieve information over long sequences, helping maintain context across extensive texts.

3. Recurrent Neural Networks (RNNs) with Attention

While traditional RNNs suffer from vanishing gradients, limiting their ability to maintain context over long sequences, the introduction of attention mechanisms has mitigated this issue. Attention mechanisms allow the model to weigh the importance of different parts of the input sequence, ensuring that relevant context is retained and emphasized even in lengthy texts.

4. Transformers and Self-Attention

Transformers, with their self-attention mechanism, have revolutionized NLP by enabling models to consider the entire input sequence simultaneously, rather than sequentially. This global perspective helps maintain context over long text generations, as the model can dynamically adjust the focus based on the entire input sequence.

5. Pointer Networks

Pointer networks are a type of model that can generate sequences by "pointing" to positions in the input sequence. This mechanism helps maintain context by directly referencing parts of the input text during generation, ensuring that the output remains relevant to the initial input.

6. Dialogue State Tracking

In conversational AI, dialogue state tracking (DST) involves maintaining a structured representation of the dialogue context. DST models keep track of the user's intents, entities mentioned, and the dialogue history, enabling the system to generate responses that are contextually appropriate and coherent over long interactions.

7. Contextual Embeddings

Contextual embeddings, such as those produced by BERT (Bidirectional Encoder Representations from Transformers) or GPT (Generative Pre-trained Transformer), capture the meaning of words in their specific context. These embeddings are crucial for maintaining context in long text generation, as they allow the model to generate text that is sensitive to the nuances and specificities of the input context.

8. Utilizing External Knowledge Bases

Incorporating external knowledge bases or databases can enhance the model's ability to maintain context by providing additional information that supplements the input text. This approach is particularly useful in domain-specific applications where maintaining context involves referencing specialized knowledge.

9. Chunking and Summarization Techniques

For extremely long texts, chunking the input into manageable segments and summarizing each segment can help maintain context. By generating summaries and focusing on key points, the model can retain the overall narrative or discussion thread, even over extensive text lengths.

Addressing Ambiguity in User Inputs

Ambiguity in user inputs poses a significant challenge in NLP. Ambiguity can arise from various factors, including homonyms, polysemy, unclear references, and incomplete information. Here are strategies to address ambiguity effectively:

1. Disambiguation Using Contextual Clues

Using contextual clues from the surrounding text can often resolve ambiguity. By analyzing the context in which an ambiguous term or phrase appears, the model can infer the most likely meaning. For instance, the word "bank" could mean a financial institution or the side of a river, but the surrounding words usually clarify the intended meaning.

2. User Clarification Requests

When faced with ambiguous inputs, prompting the user for clarification is a straightforward and effective strategy. This approach involves asking follow-up questions to gather more information, thereby reducing ambiguity. For example, if a user says, "Book a table," the system might ask, "Do you mean at a restaurant or for an event?"

3. Leveraging Pre-trained Language Models

Pre-trained language models, such as BERT or GPT-3, have been trained on vast amounts of text data and possess a nuanced understanding of language. These models can often disambiguate terms based on their extensive training. Fine-tuning these models on specific datasets can further enhance their ability to resolve ambiguity in particular domains.

4. Word Sense Disambiguation (WSD)

Word Sense Disambiguation (WSD) is a specialized technique in NLP aimed at determining which sense of a word is being used in a given context. Various algorithms, such as Lesk, machine learning-based methods, and neural approaches, can be employed to perform WSD, thereby addressing ambiguity.

5. Entity Recognition and Linking

Named Entity Recognition (NER) and Entity Linking are techniques used to identify and disambiguate entities in text. NER identifies entities such as names, dates, and locations, while Entity Linking connects these entities to a knowledge base, providing additional context and resolving ambiguities.

6. Paraphrasing and Rephrasing

Generating paraphrases of the ambiguous input can sometimes make the intended meaning clearer. This technique involves rephrasing the input in different ways and selecting the version that best fits the context. Paraphrasing can also be used to present multiple interpretations to the user for confirmation.

7. Probabilistic Models

Probabilistic models, such as Bayesian networks, can be used to handle ambiguity by representing the uncertainty in the input. These models assign probabilities to different interpretations based on contextual clues and prior knowledge, allowing the system to choose the most likely meaning.

8. Semantic Parsing

Semantic parsing involves converting natural language into a structured representation, such as a logical form or a query. By understanding the underlying semantics of the input, the system can better handle ambiguous phrases and generate more accurate responses.

9. Contextual Coherence Checking

Ensuring that the generated text or response is contextually coherent can help address ambiguity. If the generated output does not fit well with the preceding context, it might indicate that the input was ambiguous. In such cases, the system can revisit the input and attempt to resolve the ambiguity before generating a final response.

10. User Profile and History Utilization

Using information from the user's profile and interaction history can help resolve ambiguity by providing additional context. For example, knowing the user's preferences, past interactions, and specific domain knowledge can guide the interpretation of ambiguous inputs.

Handling ambiguity and maintaining context over long text generation are essential challenges in the field of natural language processing. Strategies such as hierarchical attention mechanisms, memory-augmented neural networks, and transformers help maintain context, while techniques like disambiguation using contextual clues, user clarification requests, and leveraging pre-trained language models address ambiguity.

By employing these strategies, NLP systems can generate more coherent, relevant, and accurate text, enhancing their utility in various applications, from conversational agents to complex document generation. The ongoing advancements in NLP and the integration of sophisticated techniques promise to further improve the handling of ambiguity and context, making these systems increasingly effective and reliable.

Chapter 20 LLMs in Customer Service

Large Language Models (LLMs), such as GPT-4 developed by OpenAI, represent a significant advancement in the field of artificial intelligence (AI). These models are designed to understand and generate human-like text, making them particularly useful in customer service. By automating customer interactions, LLMs can enhance efficiency, improve customer satisfaction, and provide 24/7 support. However, integrating LLMs into customer service also presents several challenges that need to be addressed to maximize their benefits.

Automating Customer Interactions

1. Understanding Customer Queries

One of the primary applications of LLMs in customer service is the ability to understand and process customer queries. LLMs are trained on vast amounts of text data, enabling them to recognize and interpret the nuances of human language. This capability allows them to understand various customer inquiries, ranging from simple requests like order status updates to more complex issues like troubleshooting technical problems.

For example, a customer may ask, "Why hasn't my order arrived yet?" An LLM can interpret this query, access the relevant order information from the database, and provide an accurate response. This automation reduces the need for human agents to handle routine inquiries, allowing them to focus on more complex tasks.

2. Generating Contextual Responses

Once an LLM understands a customer query, it can generate a relevant and contextual response. Unlike traditional chatbots, which rely on predefined scripts, LLMs can generate responses dynamically based on the context of the conversation. This ability to produce human-like responses helps create a more natural and engaging interaction with customers.

For instance, if a customer expresses dissatisfaction with a product, an LLM can offer an apology, suggest solutions, or escalate the issue to a human agent if necessary. This level of responsiveness can significantly enhance the customer experience by providing timely and personalized support.

3. Handling Multilingual Support

LLMs are also proficient in handling multilingual customer interactions. With the ability to understand and generate text in multiple languages, LLMs can cater to a global customer base. This multilingual capability is particularly valuable for companies operating in diverse markets, as it allows them to provide consistent and effective support regardless of the customer's language.

For example, a customer from Spain can receive support in Spanish, while a customer from Japan can interact in Japanese. This capability not only improves customer satisfaction but also expands the company's reach and accessibility.

Benefits of LLMs in Customer Service

1. Improved Efficiency

One of the most significant benefits of using LLMs in customer service is improved efficiency. By automating routine interactions, LLMs can handle a large volume of inquiries simultaneously, reducing wait times for customers. This efficiency is particularly beneficial during peak times when the volume of customer queries is high.

For example, during a product launch or holiday season, the number of customer inquiries can spike dramatically. LLMs can manage this increased demand effectively, ensuring that customers receive prompt responses without overwhelming human agents.

2. Cost Savings

Automating customer interactions with LLMs can lead to substantial cost savings for businesses. By reducing the reliance on human agents for routine inquiries, companies can lower their operational costs. Additionally, LLMs can operate 24/7 without the need for breaks or shifts, providing continuous support and further enhancing cost efficiency.

These cost savings can be reinvested into other areas of the business, such as product development or marketing, driving overall growth and profitability.

3. Enhanced Customer Experience

LLMs can significantly enhance the customer experience by providing quick and accurate responses. The ability to generate human-like text ensures that customers feel understood and valued. Furthermore, the consistency and reliability of LLMs can build trust and loyalty among customers.

For instance, a customer who receives a prompt and helpful response to their query is more likely to have a positive perception of the company. This positive experience can lead to repeat business and positive word-of-mouth recommendations.

4. Scalability

As businesses grow, the demand for customer support also increases. LLMs offer a scalable solution to this challenge. Unlike human agents, who require training and management, LLMs can be easily scaled to handle an increasing number of inquiries. This scalability ensures that customer support operations can keep pace with business growth without compromising on quality.

For example, a startup that experiences rapid growth can leverage LLMs to maintain high levels of customer support without the need to hire and train a large number of new agents.

Challenges of LLMs in Customer Service

1. Understanding Complex Queries

While LLMs are proficient at handling routine inquiries, they may struggle with complex or ambiguous queries. Human agents possess the ability to understand context, read between the lines, and provide nuanced responses. LLMs, on the other hand, may misinterpret complex queries or provide generic responses that do not fully address the customer's issue. For example, a customer with a technical problem that requires detailed troubleshooting may not receive adequate support from an LLM. In such cases, the issue may need to be escalated to a human agent for resolution.

2. Handling Emotional Interactions

Customer service often involves managing emotional interactions, especially when customers are frustrated or upset. Human agents are trained to handle such situations with empathy and understanding. While LLMs can be programmed to recognize certain emotional cues, they may lack the ability to respond with genuine empathy.

For instance, a customer who is angry about a delayed shipment may require a human agent to provide a reassuring and empathetic response. An LLM, despite generating an apologetic response, may not convey the same level of empathy and understanding.

3. Data Privacy and Security

The use of LLMs in customer service raises important

questions about data privacy and security. LLMs require access to customer data to provide accurate and personalized responses. However, this access must be carefully managed to protect sensitive information and comply with data protection regulations.

For example, storing and processing customer data in compliance with regulations like the General Data Protection Regulation (GDPR) is critical. Companies must ensure that LLMs are designed and implemented with robust security measures to prevent data breaches and unauthorized access.

4. Maintaining Human Oversight

While LLMs can automate many aspects of customer service, human oversight remains essential. Human agents are needed to handle complex queries, manage emotional interactions, and ensure the overall quality of customer support.

Maintaining a balance between automation and human oversight is crucial to providing a seamless and effective customer service experience.

For instance, implementing a system where LLMs handle routine inquiries while human agents focus on more complex issues can optimize the benefits of both automation and human expertise.

Future Directions

The integration of LLMs in customer service is an evolving field with significant potential for future advancements. As LLMs continue to improve in their ability to understand and generate human-like text, their role in customer service is likely to expand. Here are some potential future directions:

1. Enhanced Emotional Intelligence

Future LLMs may be equipped with improved emotional intelligence, allowing them to recognize and respond to a wider range of emotional cues. This enhancement could enable LLMs to handle emotional interactions more effectively, providing empathetic and supportive responses.

2. Better Understanding of Context

Advancements in AI research may lead to LLMs with a better understanding of context. These models could interpret complex queries more accurately, providing more relevant and precise responses. This improvement would further reduce the need for human intervention in complex cases.

3. Integration with Other Technologies

LLMs could be integrated with other emerging technologies, such as voice recognition and augmented reality, to create more interactive and immersive customer service experiences. For example, combining LLMs with voice recognition technology could enable voice-based customer support, allowing customers to interact with the system using natural speech.

4. Personalized Customer Service

Future LLMs could leverage advanced data analytics to provide highly personalized customer service. By analyzing customer behavior and preferences, LLMs could tailor responses and recommendations to individual customers, enhancing the overall customer experience.

The use of Large Language Models in customer service offers numerous benefits, including improved efficiency, cost savings, enhanced customer experience, and scalability. However, there are also challenges to address, such as understanding complex queries, handling emotional interactions, ensuring data privacy and security, and maintaining human oversight. As technology continues to advance, the role of LLMs in customer service is likely to expand, offering even more sophisticated and personalized support options. Balancing the strengths of LLMs with the irreplaceable value of human empathy and expertise will be key to achieving the best outcomes in customer service automation.

Chapter 21 Content Creation and Journalism

LLMs can significantly enhance productivity in content creation and journalism. By automating routine tasks such as drafting articles, generating headlines, and summarizing information, journalists and content creators can focus more on critical and creative aspects of their work. For instance, an LLM can quickly generate a draft of a news article based on a set of facts or data points, which a journalist can then refine and enrich with additional context and insights.

Content Personalization and Audience Engagement

Another advantage of LLMs is their ability to personalize content. By analyzing user data and preferences, LLMs can generate content tailored to specific audiences, enhancing reader engagement. Personalized content can range from recommending articles to crafting targeted newsletters and social media posts, ensuring that readers receive information that aligns with their interests.

Expanding Creative Possibilities

LLMs also open up new creative possibilities. They can assist writers in brainstorming ideas, overcoming writer's block, and exploring different writing styles. For example, a novelist might use an LLM to generate plot ideas or dialogue, while a marketing team could use it to create catchy slogans and campaign content. The versatility of LLMs in generating diverse types of content makes them invaluable in various creative domains.

Accuracy and Fact-Checking

One of the primary ethical concerns with using LLMs in journalism is ensuring the accuracy of the generated content. While LLMs are proficient at producing coherent and contextually appropriate text, they can sometimes generate inaccurate or misleading information. This issue is particularly critical in journalism, where the dissemination of false information can have serious consequences.

To address this, it is essential to implement robust fact-checking mechanisms. Journalists and editors must verify the information generated by LLMs before publication. Additionally, developing LLMs with built-in fact-checking capabilities could enhance their reliability. However, the

256

responsibility ultimately lies with human overseers to ensure the accuracy and integrity of the content.

Transparency and Disclosure

Transparency is another crucial ethical consideration. Audiences have the right to know when they are reading content generated by an LLM rather than a human author. This transparency builds trust and allows readers to critically assess the information they consume. Media organizations should clearly disclose the use of LLMs in content creation, either through bylines, disclaimers, or other appropriate means.

Bias and Fairness

LLMs are trained on vast datasets that reflect the biases

present in their source material. Consequently, they can inadvertently perpetuate or even amplify these biases in their generated content. This bias can manifest in various ways, including the underrepresentation of certain groups, the reinforcement of stereotypes, or the skewing of facts.

To mitigate this, it is vital to continuously evaluate and refine the datasets used to train LLMs, ensuring they are diverse and representative. Additionally, implementing algorithms to detect and correct biased outputs can help promote fairness in automated journalism. Media organizations must also remain vigilant and critical of the content produced by LLMs, addressing any bias that may arise.

Accountability and Responsibility

Determining accountability in automated journalism is

complex. If an LLM generates false or harmful content, who is responsible? Is it the developers of the LLM, the organization using it, or the editors overseeing the content? Clear guidelines and frameworks need to be established to delineate accountability in such scenarios.

Organizations using LLMs should implement rigorous editorial standards and oversight to ensure the quality and ethical integrity of the content. This oversight includes regular audits of the LLM's outputs and continuous training for journalists and editors on the ethical use of AI tools.

LLMs rely on vast amounts of data to function effectively, raising concerns about privacy and data security. The data used to train these models often include personal information, which, if not handled properly, can lead to privacy violations. Ensuring that data used for training LLMs is anonymized and securely stored is paramount.

Furthermore, media organizations must adhere to data

protection regulations and ethical standards when collecting

and using data for content personalization. Clear policies and

practices should be in place to safeguard user data and

maintain the trust of audiences.

Balancing Automation and Human Creativity

While LLMs offer numerous benefits in content creation and

journalism, it is essential to strike a balance between

automation and human creativity. LLMs can handle repetitive

and time-consuming tasks, allowing human journalists to

focus on investigative reporting, in-depth analysis, and

storytelling. However, the unique human touch in

interpreting events, providing context, and connecting

emotionally with audiences remains irreplaceable.

The integration of large language models into content

creation and journalism presents both exciting opportunities and significant ethical challenges. LLMs can enhance productivity, personalize content, and expand creative possibilities. However, ensuring accuracy, transparency, fairness, accountability, and data security is crucial in leveraging these tools responsibly.

As the field of automated journalism evolves, it is imperative to develop and adhere to ethical guidelines that address these concerns. By doing so, media organizations can harness the potential of LLMs while upholding the integrity and trustworthiness of journalism. Ultimately, the responsible use of LLMs can enrich the journalistic landscape, providing audiences with high-quality, engaging, and reliable content.

Looking ahead, the role of LLMs in content creation and journalism is likely to expand further, driven by advancements in AI technology and increasing demand for efficient content production. However, several key areas require ongoing attention and development:

Continuous Improvement of LLMs

The development of more advanced and nuanced LLMs is essential. Researchers and developers should focus on enhancing the models' ability to understand context, reduce biases, and improve accuracy. Incorporating real-time feedback mechanisms where LLMs learn from their mistakes and adapt to changing information can further enhance their reliability.

Ethical AI Frameworks

Establishing comprehensive ethical frameworks for the use of

AI in journalism is critical. These frameworks should be developed collaboratively by AI experts, journalists, ethicists, and policymakers. They should address issues such as data privacy, bias mitigation, accountability, and the ethical use of AI-generated content. Regular updates to these frameworks will be necessary to keep pace with technological advancements and societal changes.

Education and Training

Educating journalists, editors, and content creators about the capabilities and limitations of LLMs is vital. Training programs should focus on how to effectively use LLMs while adhering to ethical standards. Understanding the potential pitfalls and ethical dilemmas associated with AI-generated content will empower professionals to make informed decisions and maintain journalistic integrity.

Public Awareness and Engagement

Raising public awareness about the use of LLMs in content creation and journalism is also important. Engaging with audiences through transparency and open communication can help build trust. Media organizations should actively involve their readers in discussions about the role of AI in journalism, addressing concerns and gathering feedback to improve practices.

Collaboration Between AI and Human Journalists

Fostering collaboration between AI tools and human journalists can lead to more innovative and impactful journalism. AI can assist in data analysis, trend identification, and content generation, while human journalists provide critical thinking, contextual understanding, and ethical judgment. This symbiotic relationship can enhance the overall quality **and depth of journalistic work.**

The integration of large language models into content creation and journalism marks a transformative period for the industry.

While LLMs offer numerous benefits in terms of efficiency, personalization, and creativity, their use must be guided by robust ethical considerations. Ensuring accuracy, transparency, fairness, accountability, and data security is paramount in maintaining the integrity of journalism.

As technology continues to evolve, so too must our ethical frameworks and practices.

By prioritizing responsible AI usage and fostering collaboration between humans and machines, we can harness the full potential of LLMs to enrich the journalistic landscape. The future of journalism lies in the balance between innovation and ethical responsibility, ensuring that the pursuit

of efficiency and creativity does not compromise the core

values of truth, integrity, and trust.

Chapter 22 Healthcare Applications

Healthcare is a vital sector, continually evolving with advancements in technology. Among these advancements, large language models (LLMs) have emerged as transformative tools in medical research and patient interaction. These models, powered by artificial intelligence (AI), offer significant potential to improve healthcare delivery, enhance patient outcomes, and streamline medical research. However, their deployment comes with critical challenges, particularly regarding accuracy and privacy. This paper explores the applications of LLMs in healthcare, focusing on their roles in medical research and patient interaction, while also addressing the crucial aspects of ensuring accuracy and privacy.

LLMs in Medical Research

LLMs are revolutionizing medical research by enhancing the ability to analyze vast amounts of data. Traditionally, data analysis in medical research required significant manual effort, time, and expertise. LLMs, however, can process and interpret large datasets quickly and accurately, identifying patterns and insights that might be missed by human researchers. For instance, in genomics, LLMs can analyze genetic data to identify potential links between genetic markers and diseases, accelerating the discovery of new treatments and therapies.

Literature Review and Summarization

Medical research involves extensive literature reviews to keep up with the latest developments and to build upon existing knowledge. LLMs can significantly expedite this process by summarizing large volumes of scientific literature. They can extract key findings, methodologies, and conclusions from numerous papers, providing researchers with concise and comprehensive overviews. This capability not only saves time but also ensures that researchers have access to the most relevant information, facilitating more informed and effective research.

Drug Discovery

The drug discovery process is notoriously time-consuming and expensive, often taking years and billions of dollars to bring a new drug to market. LLMs can accelerate this process by predicting the interactions between drugs and biological targets. By analyzing existing drug data and biological pathways, LLMs can suggest new compounds that might be effective against specific diseases. This predictive capability helps narrow down the list of potential drugs, reducing the time and cost associated with experimental testing.

LLMs in Patient Interaction

LLMs are increasingly being used to develop virtual health assistants, which can interact with patients through natural language processing (NLP). These virtual assistants can provide patients with instant answers to their health-related queries, offer medical advice, and assist in scheduling appointments. For example, a virtual health assistant could help a patient understand their symptoms and suggest whether they need to see a doctor, thereby improving access to healthcare and reducing the burden on medical professionals.

Telemedicine

Telemedicine has gained significant traction, especially during the COVID-19 pandemic. LLMs enhance telemedicine platforms by providing real-time language translation, ensuring effective communication between patients and healthcare providers who speak different languages. Additionally, LLMs can transcribe and summarize telemedicine consultations, creating accurate medical records and freeing up clinicians to focus more on patient care rather than administrative tasks.

Personalized Patient Education

Educating patients about their conditions and treatment options is crucial for effective healthcare delivery. LLMs can personalize patient education by providing information tailored to an individual's specific condition, treatment plan, and preferences. By analyzing patient data, LLMs can generate customized educational materials that are easy to understand, helping patients make informed decisions about their health and adhere to their treatment plans.

Ensuring Accuracy in Healthcare Applications

Ensuring the accuracy of LLMs in healthcare applications is paramount. These models must be rigorously validated and verified before deployment. Validation involves testing the model on diverse datasets to ensure it performs well across different scenarios and patient populations. Verification, on the other hand, entails ensuring that the model's outputs are consistent with established medical knowledge and standards. This process often requires collaboration between AI developers and medical professionals to identify and correct any inaccuracies or biases in the model.

Continuous Monitoring and Updating

LLMs in healthcare must be continuously monitored and updated to maintain their accuracy. Medical knowledge and standards evolve over time, and models need to be updated accordingly. Continuous monitoring involves regularly assessing the model's performance and making adjustments as needed. This can include retraining the model with new data, fine-tuning its algorithms, and incorporating feedback from healthcare providers and patients. Such iterative improvements ensure that the model remains accurate and relevant.

Human-in-the-Loop Systems

To mitigate the risk of errors, many healthcare applications of

LLMs employ human-in-the-loop systems. In these systems, the LLMs provide recommendations or analyses that are reviewed and validated by medical professionals before any action is taken. This approach combines the efficiency of AI with the expertise of human clinicians, ensuring that decisions are both accurate and clinically sound. For example, an LLM might analyze patient data to suggest a potential diagnosis, which a doctor would then review and confirm.

Ensuring Privacy in Healthcare Applications

Privacy is a critical concern when using LLMs in healthcare, as these models often require access to sensitive patient data. One of the primary methods to ensure privacy is data anonymization. This process involves removing or obfuscating personally identifiable information (PII) from datasets before they are used to train or run LLMs. Techniques such as data masking, pseudonymization, and aggregation help protect patient identities while still allowing the models to extract valuable insights from the data.

Secure Data Storage and Transmission

Ensuring the privacy of patient data also involves secure data storage and transmission. Healthcare organizations must implement robust encryption protocols to protect data at rest and in transit. This includes using advanced encryption standards (AES) for data storage and secure sockets layer (SSL)/transport layer security (TLS) for data transmission. Additionally, access controls and authentication mechanisms should be in place to ensure that only authorized personnel can access sensitive data.

Compliance with Regulations

Healthcare applications of LLMs must comply with relevant

privacy regulations, such as the Health Insurance Portability and Accountability Act (HIPAA) in the United States and the General Data Protection Regulation (GDPR) in the European Union. These regulations set stringent requirements for the protection of personal data, including the need for explicit patient consent, the right to data access and deletion, and the obligation to report data breaches. Compliance with these regulations is essential to ensure that patient privacy is maintained and that healthcare organizations avoid legal penalties.

Addressing Bias in LLMs

One of the significant challenges in deploying LLMs in healthcare is addressing bias. Bias in AI models can arise from various sources, including the training data, model algorithms, and human oversight. In healthcare, biased models can lead to disparities in treatment and outcomes, particularly for underrepresented populations. To address this issue, it is crucial to use diverse and representative training datasets, implement bias detection and mitigation techniques, and involve diverse stakeholders in the model development process.

Enhancing Model Interpretability

Another challenge is enhancing the interpretability of LLMs. In healthcare, it is not enough for a model to provide accurate predictions or recommendations; clinicians need to understand the reasoning behind these outputs. Enhancing interpretability involves developing methods that allow models to explain their decisions in a way that is understandable to medical professionals. Techniques such as attention mechanisms, feature importance analysis, and explainable AI (XAI) frameworks can help achieve this goal.

Integrating LLMs into Clinical Workflow

Integrating LLMs into clinical workflows presents both technical and organizational challenges. Technically, LLMs need to be compatible with existing electronic health record (EHR) systems and other healthcare IT infrastructure. Organizationally, there needs to be buy-in from healthcare providers, who may be resistant to adopting new technologies. Effective integration requires collaboration between AI developers, healthcare IT professionals, and clinicians to ensure that the models are user-friendly, reliable, and seamlessly integrated into daily practice.

The applications of LLMs in healthcare are vast and hold tremendous potential to transform medical research and patient interaction. By enhancing data analysis, expediting literature reviews, and accelerating drug discovery, LLMs can significantly advance medical research. In patient interaction,

LLMs can improve access to healthcare, enhance communication, and personalize patient education. However, the deployment of these models comes with critical challenges related to accuracy and privacy. Ensuring accuracy requires rigorous validation, continuous monitoring, and human oversight, while ensuring privacy involves data anonymization, secure storage and transmission, and regulatory compliance. Addressing these challenges and continually improving the technology will be essential to fully realizing the potential of LLMs in healthcare. As we move forward, it will be crucial to address bias, enhance interpretability, and ensure seamless integration into clinical workflows to ensure that these powerful tools are used effectively and ethically in the healthcare sector.

Chapter 23 Education and E-Learning

The landscape of education has experienced a transformative shift with the advent of digital technologies. E-learning, facilitated by internet accessibility and advanced software, has redefined the way knowledge is disseminated and acquired. Central to this transformation is the role of Large Language Models (LLMs) in creating personalized learning experiences. These models, powered by artificial intelligence (AI), enable tailored educational experiences that cater to individual learning styles and needs. This essay explores the impact of LLMs on personalized learning and presents case studies that highlight the efficacy of educational technology.

The Emergence of Personalized Learning with LLMs

Large Language Models are AI systems designed to understand and generate human-like text. Trained on vast datasets, these models can comprehend context, provide detailed explanations, and engage in meaningful dialogue with users. Notable examples include OpenAI's GPT-3 and its successors, which have demonstrated remarkable capabilities in various domains, including education.

Personalized Learning Defined

Personalized learning refers to instructional approaches that tailor education to individual learners' needs, preferences, and interests. This method contrasts with traditional one-size-fits-all teaching models, aiming instead to optimize learning outcomes by addressing the unique attributes of each student.

LLMs and Personalized Learning

LLMs facilitate personalized learning by providing customized educational content and feedback. They can adapt to the learner's pace, offer additional explanations for complex topics, and suggest resources that align with the learner's interests. This dynamic adaptability makes LLMs an invaluable tool in creating engaging and effective learning environments.

Benefits of LLMs in Education

Adaptive Learning Paths

LLMs can analyze a learner's performance and adjust the difficulty of tasks accordingly. For instance, if a student struggles with a particular concept, the model can provide additional practice problems or alternative explanations.

Conversely, for advanced learners, LLMs can introduce more challenging material to keep them engaged.

Instant Feedback and Assessment

Immediate feedback is crucial for effective learning. LLMs can evaluate students' responses in real time, offering instant corrections and explanations. This immediate interaction helps students understand their mistakes and learn from them promptly, which is more effective than waiting for feedback from a human instructor.

Enhanced Accessibility

LLMs can break down barriers to education by providing support in multiple languages and accommodating various learning disabilities. For example, they can convert text to speech, provide subtitles, and offer explanations in simpler language, making learning more inclusive.

Continuous Engagement

Engaging students consistently is a challenge in education. LLMs can create interactive and immersive learning experiences through simulations, quizzes, and conversational agents. These tools maintain student interest and encourage active participation in the learning process.

Case Studies in Educational Technology

Case Study 1: Khan Academy and AI Integration

Khan Academy, a pioneer in online education, has integrated AI to enhance personalized learning. Utilizing LLMs, the platform offers tailored learning experiences to millions of students worldwide. The AI system assesses students' strengths and weaknesses, providing customized practice exercises and instructional videos.

Impact: Students using the AI-powered Khan Academy platform show significant improvements in their learning outcomes. The adaptive learning paths ensure that each student receives the right level of challenge and support, leading to better retention and understanding of concepts.

Case Study 2: Duolingo's Personalized Language Learning

Duolingo, a popular language-learning app, employs LLMs to create personalized learning experiences. The app adapts to the user's proficiency level, offering customized lessons and practice sessions. It also provides instant feedback on pronunciation and grammar, helping users improve their language skills effectively.

Impact: Duolingo's use of LLMs has made language learning accessible and engaging for millions of users. The personalized approach ensures that learners remain motivated and achieve better outcomes compared to traditional language courses.

Case Study 3: Carnegie Learning's Cognitive Tutor

Carnegie Learning developed a cognitive tutor system that uses AI to personalize math instruction. The system assesses students' problem-solving processes and provides targeted feedback and hints. It also adjusts the difficulty of problems based on the student's performance.

Impact: Schools implementing Carnegie Learning's cognitive tutor have reported improved math scores and a deeper understanding of mathematical concepts among students. The personalized feedback and adaptive learning paths contribute significantly to these positive outcomes.

Case Study 4: Coursera's Adaptive Learning Platform

Coursera, a leading provider of online courses, has integrated

LLMs to enhance its adaptive learning platform. The AI system analyzes learners' interactions with course material and adjusts the content delivery accordingly. It provides personalized recommendations for additional resources and practice exercises.

Impact: Coursera's adaptive learning platform has increased learner engagement and completion rates. By tailoring the learning experience to individual needs, the platform helps students stay motivated and achieve their learning goals.

Data Privacy and Security

The use of LLMs in education involves handling vast amounts of personal data. Ensuring data privacy and security is paramount to protect students' information. Educational institutions and technology providers must implement robust data protection measures and comply with relevant regulations.

287

Equity and Access

While LLMs offer significant benefits, ensuring equitable access to these technologies remains a challenge. Disparities in internet access and digital literacy can hinder the widespread adoption of personalized learning tools. Efforts to bridge the digital divide are essential to ensure that all students can benefit from these advancements.

Ethical Considerations

The deployment of AI in education raises ethical questions regarding the potential biases in LLMs. These models are trained on large datasets that may contain biases, which can be inadvertently perpetuated in their outputs. Continuous monitoring and updating of these models are necessary to mitigate bias and ensure fair treatment of all learners.

Teacher Training and Support

Integrating LLMs into the educational system requires training and support for educators. Teachers must be equipped with the knowledge and skills to effectively use these technologies in their classrooms. Professional development programs and resources are crucial to help educators adapt to the changing educational landscape.

Advancements in AI and LLMs

As AI technology continues to advance, LLMs will become even more sophisticated, offering deeper insights into students' learning processes. Future models will likely provide more nuanced feedback, support a wider range of subjects, and facilitate collaborative learning experiences.

Integration with Augmented and Virtual Reality

The integration of LLMs with augmented reality (AR) and virtual reality (VR) can create immersive learning environments. These technologies can simulate real-world scenarios, allowing students to apply their knowledge in practical contexts. This combination has the potential to revolutionize fields such as medical training, engineering, and more.

Lifelong Learning and Workforce Development

LLMs can play a significant role in lifelong learning and workforce development. As industries evolve, continuous learning becomes essential. AI-powered personalized learning platforms can help individuals acquire new skills and stay competitive in the job market.

Collaborative Learning and Peer Interaction

Future educational technologies will likely focus on enhancing collaborative learning experiences. LLMs can facilitate group discussions, peer reviews, and collaborative projects, fostering a sense of community and encouraging knowledge sharing among students.

The integration of Large Language Models into education marks a significant advancement in personalized learning. These models provide adaptive learning paths, instant feedback, and enhanced accessibility, transforming traditional educational paradigms. Case studies from platforms like Khan Academy, Duolingo, Carnegie Learning, and Coursera demonstrate the tangible benefits of LLMs in improving learning outcomes. However, challenges such as data privacy, equity, and ethical considerations must be addressed to fully realize the potential of these technologies. As AI continues to evolve, the future of education promises even more innovative and effective learning experiences, making lifelong learning a reality for all.

Chapter 24 Multimodal Models

Multimodal models represent a fascinating and rapidly advancing area of artificial intelligence (AI). These models integrate different types of data—such as text, images, and even audio—into a single coherent framework. The primary goal of multimodal models is to leverage the complementary strengths of various data types to achieve a richer understanding and more powerful generation capabilities than would be possible with unimodal data alone. This capability has profound implications for numerous applications, including image generation, search engines, accessibility technologies, and more.

The Importance of Multimodal Models

Understanding and interpreting the world requires synthesizing information from multiple sensory modalities. Humans naturally combine visual, auditory, and textual information to perceive and interact with their environment. AI systems aim to replicate this human ability, allowing for more intuitive interactions and richer data processing capabilities.

By integrating multiple modalities, these models can:

1. Improve Understanding: Combining text and image data can lead to a deeper understanding than considering each modality separately. For instance, an image with a descriptive

caption can convey more information than either the image or the caption alone.

2. Enhance Performance: Multimodal models often outperform unimodal models on various tasks. For example, in tasks like image captioning, visual question answering, and text-to-image generation, leveraging both text and images can lead to better results.

3. Enable New Applications: Multimodal models open up possibilities for innovative applications, such as generating images from textual descriptions, translating text in images, and creating more interactive AI systems that can understand and generate content across different modalities.

Integrating Text with Images and Other Modalities

Integrating multiple modalities involves creating representations that can effectively combine information from different sources. This integration can occur at various stages of the model architecture, including input, intermediate representation, and output stages.

Input-Level Integration: This approach involves directly combining raw inputs from different modalities. For example, in a model designed to analyze multimedia documents, text and image inputs can be fed into the model simultaneously, allowing it to learn joint representations from the start.

Representation-Level Integration: Here, separate neural networks process each modality independently to generate high-level representations, which are then combined. This method allows the model to first understand each modality in its own right before integrating the information. Techniques like attention mechanisms can be used to weigh the importance of each modality's contribution.

Output-Level Integration: In this approach, the model generates outputs for each modality separately, which are then combined to produce a final result. For example, in a text-to-image generation task, the model might generate textual descriptions and visual elements separately and then merge them into a coherent image.

Examples of Multimodal Models

CLIP (Contrastive Language-Image Pretraining)

CLIP, developed by OpenAI, is a prominent example of a multimodal model that integrates text and images. CLIP's architecture and training methodology represent significant advancements in the field of multimodal learning.

Architecture and Training: CLIP is trained using a contrastive learning approach, where the model learns to associate text descriptions with corresponding images. It consists of two encoders: one for text and one for images. The encoders map text and images into a shared embedding space, where the similarity between text and image pairs is maximized, and the similarity between mismatched pairs is minimized.

Applications: CLIP can perform a wide range of tasks without task-specific fine-tuning. These tasks include image classification, zero-shot learning, and text-based image retrieval. For instance, given a textual query, CLIP can retrieve the most relevant images from a large dataset, demonstrating its powerful capability to understand and link text and image data.

Impact: CLIP's ability to generalize across various tasks without additional training has significant implications for the scalability and adaptability of AI systems. It represents a step toward creating more versatile and robust AI models capable of handling diverse real-world scenarios.

DALL-E

DALL-E, another groundbreaking model from OpenAI, extends the capabilities of multimodal models by focusing on generating images from textual descriptions. This ability to create visual content from text has wide-ranging applications, from creative industries to enhancing accessibility.

Architecture and Training: DALL-E is based on the GPT-3 architecture, adapted for image generation. It uses a transformer network to generate images from textual prompts. During training, DALL-E learns to map sequences of text tokens to sequences of image tokens, effectively learning the relationship between textual descriptions and visual content.

Applications: DALL-E can generate a diverse array of images based on textual input, including highly specific and imaginative scenarios. For example, given a prompt like "an armchair in the shape of an avocado," DALL-E can create a visually coherent and contextually appropriate image. This capability is particularly useful in design, advertising, and entertainment, where creative visual content is in high demand.

Impact: DALL-E showcases the potential of multimodal models to enhance creativity and innovation. By translating textual ideas into visual representations, DALL-E bridges the gap between conceptualization and realization, enabling users to bring their imaginations to life with unprecedented ease.

Challenges and Future Directions

While multimodal models like CLIP and DALL-E have demonstrated impressive capabilities, several challenges remain in the development and deployment of these models. Data Quality and Bias: Multimodal models require large, high-quality datasets that accurately represent the diversity of real-world scenarios. Ensuring these datasets are free from biases is crucial to prevent the models from perpetuating harmful stereotypes or producing biased outputs. Computational Resources: Training multimodal models, especially large-scale ones like CLIP and DALL-E, demands significant computational resources. This requirement can limit access to these technologies and pose challenges for smaller research teams or organizations with limited budgets.

300

Interpretability: As multimodal models become more complex, understanding how they make decisions becomes increasingly challenging. Improving the interpretability of these models is essential for building trust and ensuring their outputs are reliable and transparent.

Integration with Other Modalities: While current models primarily focus on text and images, integrating additional modalities like audio, video, and sensor data remains an area of active research. Achieving seamless integration across multiple modalities will further enhance the versatility and applicability of these models.

Future Directions

Improving Efficiency: Developing more efficient training algorithms and model architectures can help reduce the computational burden of multimodal models. Techniques like model distillation, pruning, and quantization can make these models more accessible and scalable.

Enhanced Multimodal Interaction: Future models could enable richer interactions between different modalities, such as generating videos from text or creating immersive virtual environments based on multimodal inputs. These advancements will open up new possibilities for applications in entertainment, education, and beyond.

Personalization and Adaptability: Personalizing multimodal models to individual users' preferences and needs can improve user experience and satisfaction. Adaptive models that can learn from user interactions and feedback will be more effective in providing relevant and tailored outputs.

Ethical Considerations: Addressing ethical concerns, such as bias, privacy, and misuse, is critical for the responsible development and deployment of multimodal models. Establishing guidelines and best practices for ethical AI development will help ensure these technologies benefit society as a whole.

Multimodal models represent a significant leap forward in AI research, offering the ability to integrate and leverage information from diverse sources like text and images. Examples like CLIP and DALL-E demonstrate the power and potential of these models to revolutionize various applications, from image generation to information retrieval. While challenges remain, ongoing research and development efforts are paving the way for more efficient, interpretable, and ethical multimodal models. As these technologies continue to evolve, they hold the promise of enabling richer, more intuitive, and more powerful AI systems that can better understand and interact with the world in a human-like manner.

Chapter 25 Zero-Shot and Few-Shot Learning

In machine learning, creating models that generalize well from limited data is a significant challenge. Traditionally, models require large datasets for training to perform effectively on tasks like image classification, natural language processing, and more. However, in real-world scenarios, acquiring large annotated datasets can be impractical or impossible. This has led to the development of techniques such as zero-shot and few-shot learning, which aim to train models to perform well with minimal data.

Zero-Shot Learning

Capabilities of Zero-Shot Learning

Zero-shot learning (ZSL) enables models to make accurate predictions on classes that were not seen during the training phase. This is achieved through the use of auxiliary information that relates the unseen classes to the seen classes. Commonly, this auxiliary information includes semantic embeddings derived from textual descriptions, attribute vectors, or word embeddings.

Generalization to Unseen Classes: One of the primary capabilities of zero-shot learning is its ability to generalize to entirely new classes. For instance, if a model is trained to recognize animals using images and textual descriptions of cats, dogs, and horses, it can potentially recognize a zebra if provided with a semantic description of a zebra.

Reduction in Data Requirements: Zero-shot learning reduces

the need for extensive labeled datasets. By leveraging

semantic relationships between known and unknown classes,

models can infer characteristics of unseen classes without

direct training examples.

Flexibility Across Domains: Zero-shot learning can be

applied across various domains, including image classification,

natural language processing, and even reinforcement learning.

This flexibility makes it a powerful tool for a wide range of

applications.

Limitations of Zero-Shot Learning

Despite its potential, zero-shot learning has several

limitations:

Dependence on Quality of Semantic Information: The

accuracy of zero-shot learning models heavily relies on the

quality and comprehensiveness of the auxiliary semantic information. Poorly defined or ambiguous semantic descriptions can lead to incorrect predictions.

Scalability Issues: As the number of unseen classes increases, maintaining high accuracy becomes challenging. The model needs to differentiate between a larger number of classes based solely on semantic information, which can become complex and error-prone.

Performance Gap: Typically, zero-shot learning models do not perform as well as fully supervised models trained on large datasets. The lack of direct training examples for unseen classes often leads to a performance gap.

Few-Shot Learning

Few-shot learning (FSL) focuses on enabling models to perform well with only a small number of training examples for each class. Unlike zero-shot learning, few-shot learning assumes that at least a few labeled examples are available for each class.

Rapid Adaptation: Few-shot learning models can quickly adapt to new tasks or classes with minimal data. This is particularly useful in dynamic environments where new classes or tasks frequently emerge.

Meta-Learning: Many few-shot learning approaches use meta-learning, where the model is trained to learn how to learn. This involves training on a variety of tasks so that the model can quickly adapt to new tasks with few examples.

Efficiency: Few-shot learning significantly reduces the need for large annotated datasets, making it more practical and cost-effective in situations where data collection is expensive or time-consuming.

Limitations of Few-Shot Learning

Few-shot learning also comes with its own set of challenges:

Overfitting Risk: With limited training examples, there is a high risk of overfitting. The model might memorize the few examples rather than generalizing from them.

Complexity in Model Design: Designing effective few-shot learning models often requires complex architectures and training regimes, such as the use of neural networks that can support meta-learning or the implementation of sophisticated similarity measures.

Dependence on Pre-Trained Models: Many few-shot learning approaches rely on pre-trained models that have been trained on large datasets. This can limit their applicability in domains where such pre-trained models are not available.

Practical Applications and Examples

Image Classification: Zero-shot learning can be used for image classification tasks where obtaining labeled data for every possible category is infeasible. For example, a wildlife monitoring system might use zero-shot learning to identify rare species of animals based on textual descriptions.

Natural Language Processing: In NLP, zero-shot learning can be applied to tasks such as sentiment analysis, where a model trained on general text data can analyze sentiments in specific domains (e.g., finance or healthcare) without direct training data from those domains.

Recommendation Systems: Zero-shot learning can improve recommendation systems by predicting user preferences for new items that have not been previously interacted with. This is done by leveraging the semantic similarity between new and existing items.

Robotics: In robotics, zero-shot learning can enable robots to recognize and interact with objects that they have not encountered during training. For example, a household robot could identify and manipulate new types of utensils based on their descriptions.

Few-Shot Learning Applications

Medical Diagnosis: Few-shot learning is particularly valuable in medical diagnosis, where labeled data is often scarce. A model can be trained to recognize rare diseases with only a few examples, improving diagnostic capabilities in healthcare.

Speech Recognition: Few-shot learning can enhance speech recognition systems by allowing them to adapt to new speakers with only a few voice samples. This improves the system's robustness and personalization.

Personalized Education: In educational technology, few-shot learning can be used to develop personalized learning systems that adapt to the unique needs of each student based on limited interaction data.

Finance: In the financial industry, few-shot learning can help in fraud detection by learning to recognize new types of fraudulent activities with minimal examples, thereby improving security measures.

Case Studies

Zero-Shot Learning in ImageNet

A prominent example of zero-shot learning is its application to the ImageNet dataset. Researchers have demonstrated that zero-shot learning models can identify unseen classes in ImageNet by leveraging word embeddings from large text corpora. This approach uses semantic relationships between known and unknown classes, allowing the model to generalize beyond the training data.

Few-Shot Learning in Omniglot

The Omniglot dataset, often referred to as the "transcription test" of few-shot learning, consists of handwritten characters from various alphabets. Few-shot learning models trained on Omniglot can recognize new characters with only one or a few examples. This showcases the potential of few-shot learning in tasks requiring rapid adaptation to new categories.

Zero-shot and few-shot learning represent significant advancements in the field of machine learning, addressing the challenges posed by limited data availability. Zero-shot learning excels in generalizing to entirely unseen classes using semantic information, while few-shot learning focuses on rapid adaptation with minimal training examples. Both approaches have practical applications across diverse domains, from image classification and natural language processing to medical diagnosis and personalized education. However, they also face limitations, such as dependence on high-quality semantic information, risk of overfitting, and complexity in model design. Continued research and development in these areas hold the promise of further enhancing the capabilities and applicability of machine learning models in real-world scenarios where data is scarce.

Chapter 26 Handling Multilingual Text

Handling multilingual text in natural language processing (NLP) is a crucial area of research and application, given the diverse linguistic landscape of our world today. As communication transcends geographical and linguistic boundaries, NLP systems must be adept at understanding and processing text in multiple languages. This article explores various aspects of handling multilingual text in NLP, focusing on training models on multilingual datasets, the challenges involved, and techniques developed to address these challenges.

Training Models on Multilingual Datasets

Training models on multilingual datasets is a fundamental approach to enable NLP systems to understand and generate text in different languages. Traditionally, NLP models were often trained and evaluated on single-language corpora, which limited their applicability to specific languages. However, with the rise of global connectivity and the need for cross-linguistic understanding, the development of multilingual models has gained significant traction.

Multilingual Corpora

The cornerstone of training multilingual NLP models lies in the availability of large-scale multilingual corpora. These corpora consist of text data in multiple languages, often sourced from various domains such as news articles, social media posts, literature, and more. Creating such corpora involves significant effort in data collection, cleaning, and alignment across languages to ensure coherence and relevance.

Cross-Lingual Embeddings

One effective technique for leveraging multilingual data is the development of cross-lingual word embeddings. Embeddings like Word2Vec, GloVe, and FastText can be trained on multilingual corpora to learn representations of words that capture semantic similarities across different languages. These embeddings enable models to transfer knowledge learned from one language to another, facilitating tasks like translation, sentiment analysis, and classification in diverse linguistic contexts.

Multilingual Pretrained Models

Recent advancements in NLP have seen the emergence of multilingual pretrained models such as mBERT (multilingual BERT), XLM (Cross-lingual Language Model), and mT5 (multilingual T5). These models are pretrained on vast amounts of multilingual text, allowing them to encode and understand multiple languages simultaneously. Fine-tuning these models on specific downstream tasks further enhances their performance across different languages, making them highly versatile for multilingual applications.

Challenges in Multilingual NLP

While training models on multilingual datasets offers significant advantages, it also presents several challenges that must be addressed for robust performance across languages.

Language Imbalance

One major challenge is the imbalance in available data across languages. Some languages have abundant resources and well-annotated datasets, while others have limited resources, which can lead to skewed performance when applying NLP models across different languages. Techniques like data augmentation, synthetic data generation, and transfer learning from resource-rich languages can mitigate these disparities to some extent.

Language Divergence

Languages exhibit structural and syntactic variations that pose challenges for NLP tasks like machine translation and syntactic parsing. These differences require models to be flexible in capturing diverse linguistic patterns and nuances. Techniques such as language-specific fine-tuning and incorporating language-specific features during training can improve the adaptability of models to linguistic variations.

Code-Switching and Multilingual Context

In many multilingual communities, speakers frequently switch between languages within a single conversation or text (code-switching). This phenomenon complicates NLP tasks, as models need to accurately interpret and generate text in multiple languages within the same context. Addressing code-switching requires robust models capable of understanding and processing mixed-language input effectively.

Techniques in Multilingual NLP

To overcome the challenges associated with multilingual text, researchers have developed various techniques and methodologies tailored to the complexities of linguistic diversity.

Zero-Shot and Few-Shot Learning

Zero-shot and few-shot learning approaches enable models to generalize to unseen languages by leveraging multilingual pretrained embeddings or models. These techniques allow NLP systems to perform adequately on languages with minimal or no task-specific training data, thereby extending their applicability to low-resource languages.

Multilingual Fine-Tuning

Fine-tuning pretrained multilingual models on task-specific datasets is a common practice to enhance their performance across different languages. By fine-tuning on diverse datasets, models can learn language-specific nuances and improve their accuracy and robustness in multilingual settings.

Language-Adversarial Training

Language-adversarial training techniques aim to minimize the impact of language-specific biases during model training. By encouraging models to learn language-invariant representations, these techniques promote better generalization across languages and reduce performance disparities caused by linguistic variations.

Multilingual Data Augmentation

Data augmentation methods tailored for multilingual datasets help alleviate data scarcity issues in low-resource languages. Techniques such as back-translation, paraphrasing, and synthetic data generation generate diverse training samples, enriching the model's exposure to different linguistic contexts and improving its overall performance on multilingual tasks.

Handling multilingual text in NLP involves navigating through a diverse array of languages, each with unique linguistic characteristics and challenges. Training models on multilingual datasets, while beneficial, requires overcoming hurdles such as language imbalance, divergence, and code-switching. Through innovative techniques like multilingual embeddings, pretrained models, and language-agnostic training methods, researchers continue to advance the frontier of multilingual NLP, making significant strides towards more inclusive and effective language technologies. As global communication continues to evolve, the ability to understand and process multilingual text accurately remains pivotal for the future development of NLP applications worldwide.

Chapter 27 Understanding Bias in LLMs

Large Language Models (LLMs) represent a significant advancement in natural language processing, capable of generating coherent and contextually relevant text based on vast amounts of training data. However, like any technological innovation, they are susceptible to biases that can manifest in various forms throughout their operation. Bias in LLMs can arise from several sources, including the training data itself and the algorithms used for training and fine-tuning. This essay explores the sources of bias in LLM training data, examines case studies where bias has been observed in LLM outputs, and discusses the implications of these biases.

Sources of Bias in Training Data

Data Selection Bias: LLMs are typically trained on large datasets scraped from the internet, which inherently reflect the biases present in online sources. These biases can include cultural, geographical, and demographic biases that are embedded in the language used online.

Underrepresentation and Overrepresentation: Certain groups or topics may be underrepresented or overrepresented in the training data, leading to biases in how the model understands and generates text related to these groups or topics. For example, languages spoken by smaller populations may have less representation in training data compared to widely spoken languages.

Historical Biases: Training data often reflects historical biases present in society at the time the data was generated. This can perpetuate stereotypes and inequalities when the model learns from biased historical texts or datasets.

Labeling Bias: Datasets used to train LLMs are often labeled by humans, who themselves may have biases that influence how they categorize or annotate the data. This can introduce biases into the model's understanding of relationships between concepts or entities.

Contextual Bias: The context in which the training data was generated may not generalize well to all contexts where the LLM might be applied, leading to biased outputs in new or different contexts.

Case Studies of Bias in LLM Outputs

Gender Bias: Numerous studies have highlighted gender

biases in LLM outputs. For instance, LLMs have been found to associate stereotypical roles or characteristics with specific genders, such as linking caregiving tasks with women and leadership roles with men. This bias can influence how the model generates text related to professions, capabilities, or societal roles.

Racial Bias: LLMs trained on biased datasets have been shown to produce racially biased outputs. For example, associating certain races with criminal behavior or perpetuating racial stereotypes in text generation. This can perpetuate harmful stereotypes and contribute to discrimination.

Cultural Bias: LLMs trained predominantly on data from specific cultural contexts may struggle to generate text that is sensitive to diverse cultural perspectives or norms. This can lead to misunderstandings or misrepresentations when the model interacts with users from different cultural backgrounds.

Geographical Bias: LLMs trained on data primarily from certain regions or countries may exhibit biases in understanding or generating text related to other regions or countries. This can affect how information is perceived or communicated across different geographical contexts.

Political Bias: LLMs can inadvertently reflect political biases present in the training data, influencing how they generate text related to political topics, ideologies, or figures.

Implications of Bias in LLMs

Reinforcement of Stereotypes: Biases in LLM outputs can reinforce and perpetuate stereotypes present in society, potentially exacerbating social inequalities and discrimination.

Ethical Concerns: The ethical implications of biased LLM

outputs are significant, as they can impact decision-making processes, public opinion, and the way information is disseminated online.

User Trust and Perception: Biased outputs from LLMs can erode user trust in AI systems and affect how these systems are perceived by the general public or specific user groups.

Mitigation Strategies: Addressing bias in LLMs requires a multifaceted approach, including diversifying training data, developing algorithms to detect and mitigate biases, involving diverse stakeholders in model development, and promoting transparency in AI systems.

Regulatory Considerations: As the impact of biased LLMs becomes more apparent, there is a growing call for regulatory frameworks to ensure that AI technologies are developed and deployed responsibly, with considerations for fairness, accountability, and transparency.

While LLMs offer immense potential for enhancing natural

language understanding and generation, they are not immune to biases inherent in their training data and design. Understanding the sources of bias in LLMs, examining case studies where biases have been observed in LLM outputs, and considering the implications of these biases are crucial steps in advancing the responsible development and deployment of AI technologies. Addressing bias in LLMs requires collaboration across disciplines, ethical considerations, and ongoing efforts to mitigate biases to ensure these technologies contribute positively to society's advancement.

Chapter 28 Mitigating Bias

In recent years, the proliferation of machine learning (ML) models across various domains has brought to light significant concerns regarding bias. Bias in ML models can manifest in several forms, such as unfair treatment of certain demographic groups, perpetuation of stereotypes, or skewed decision-making processes. Addressing these biases is not just an ethical imperative but also crucial for ensuring the reliability and fairness of automated systems that increasingly influence our lives.

Techniques to Reduce Bias in Models

Data Preprocessing and Cleaning:

  - Debiasing Techniques: One approach involves

preprocessing data to mitigate biases before training the model. This can include techniques such as reweighing instances or features based on sensitive attributes like gender or race.

  - Data Augmentation: By augmenting data with synthetic examples that balance underrepresented groups, models can be trained to make more equitable predictions.

  - Data Stratification: Ensuring that training datasets are representative across different demographic groups helps in reducing bias during model training.

Algorithmic Fairness:

  - Fairness Constraints: Introducing constraints during model training to ensure that predictions do not disproportionately favor or disadvantage specific groups.

  - Fair Representation Learning: Techniques like adversarial learning or generative adversarial networks (GANs) are used to learn representations that are invariant to sensitive attributes.

Post-Processing Techniques:

- Bias Detection: Implementing methods to detect biases after model training and before deployment. This includes statistical parity measures, disparate impact analysis, and equalized odds.

- Bias Mitigation: Adjusting predictions or decision thresholds to achieve fairness without sacrificing too much on overall model performance.

Explainability and Transparency:

- Interpretable Models: Choosing models that are inherently more interpretable can aid in understanding how decisions are made, thereby identifying and mitigating biases more effectively.

- Model Documentation: Documenting model decisions, biases identified, and steps taken to mitigate them enhances transparency and accountability.

Ongoing Research and Future Directions

Advanced Fairness Metrics:

- Developing new fairness metrics that capture nuances of bias in different contexts, such as intersectional biases or temporal biases that evolve over time.

- Incorporating multiple fairness metrics simultaneously to achieve a more comprehensive assessment of model fairness.

Ethical AI Frameworks:

- Establishing ethical guidelines and frameworks that integrate bias mitigation into the entire lifecycle of AI development, from data collection to model deployment.

- Promoting interdisciplinary research collaborations between computer scientists, ethicists, social scientists, and policymakers to address ethical concerns in AI.

Bias in Reinforcement Learning:

- Addressing biases that can arise in reinforcement learning algorithms, especially in scenarios where biased training data or reward structures lead to unfair outcomes.

Diversity in Data and Model Design:

   - Encouraging diversity in data collection to ensure representation of all demographic groups, thereby reducing biases inherent in biased datasets.

   - Designing models that are inherently robust against biases by leveraging techniques like adversarial training or incorporating fairness-aware objectives.

Human-in-the-Loop Approaches:

   - Integrating human oversight and feedback loops in AI systems to continuously monitor for biases and make necessary adjustments.

   - Empowering stakeholders, including affected communities, to participate in the development and evaluation of AI systems to ensure fairness and accountability.

Global Perspectives and Regulations:

- Considering global perspectives on fairness and biases in AI, as cultural and societal norms vary widely across different regions.

- Implementing regulations and policies that mandate fairness and transparency in AI systems, ensuring adherence to ethical standards and protecting human rights.

Mitigating bias in machine learning models is a multifaceted challenge that requires a combination of technical innovation, ethical considerations, and regulatory frameworks. While significant progress has been made in developing techniques to reduce bias and enhance fairness in ML models, there remains much to be explored and implemented. Ongoing research efforts and collaborations across disciplines are crucial to advancing our understanding and capabilities in creating AI systems that are equitable, transparent, and beneficial for all stakeholders. By addressing bias proactively and systematically, we can foster trust in AI technologies and harness their potential for positive societal impact.

Chapter 29 Ethical Use of LLMs

In recent years, Large Language Models (LLMs) have emerged as powerful tools capable of generating human-like text and performing a variety of language-related tasks. These models, such as OpenAI's GPT-3, have been deployed in diverse fields including customer service, content generation, and even medical diagnostics. However, with great power comes great responsibility. The ethical implications of using LLMs are profound and multifaceted, raising concerns about privacy, bias, misinformation, and the overall impact on society. This essay explores the guidelines for responsible AI use, ethical dilemmas associated with LLMs, and strategies to address these challenges.

Guidelines for Responsible AI Use

Responsible use of LLMs involves adhering to a set of guidelines that prioritize ethical considerations over purely technical capabilities. These guidelines encompass several key principles:

Transparency and Accountability: Organizations deploying LLMs should be transparent about their use cases and ensure accountability for the outcomes generated by these models. This includes providing clear explanations of how decisions are made and who is responsible for those decisions.

Privacy and Data Security: LLMs often require vast amounts of data to train effectively. It is crucial to prioritize user privacy and implement robust data security measures to protect sensitive information from unauthorized access or misuse.

Bias Mitigation: Bias in AI systems can perpetuate and amplify societal inequalities. Developers should proactively identify and mitigate biases in LLMs, ensuring fair and equitable outcomes for all users regardless of race, gender, or other protected characteristics.

Quality and Reliability: LLMs should be continuously monitored and evaluated to maintain high standards of quality and reliability. This includes addressing issues such as accuracy, coherence, and relevance of generated content.

User Empowerment: Users interacting with LLMs should have control over their data and the ability to understand and modify the behavior of these systems to align with their preferences and values.

Ethical Review and Oversight: Establishing independent ethical review boards or committees can provide oversight and guidance on the development and deployment of LLMs, ensuring adherence to ethical standards and best practices.

Ethical Dilemmas and How to Address Them

Despite the potential benefits of LLMs, they also present several ethical dilemmas that require careful consideration and mitigation strategies:

Misinformation and Fake News: LLMs can inadvertently generate misleading or false information, which can spread rapidly and undermine public trust. Addressing this dilemma involves enhancing the model's ability to distinguish between reliable and unreliable sources and promoting media literacy among users.

Bias and Fairness: LLMs trained on biased data can perpetuate and amplify existing societal biases. To address this, developers should implement techniques such as dataset diversification, bias detection algorithms, and fairness-aware training to mitigate bias and promote fairness in AI systems.

Privacy Concerns: LLMs may inadvertently expose sensitive user information through data leaks or unauthorized access. To safeguard privacy, organizations should adopt privacy-preserving techniques such as differential privacy, federated learning, and secure multiparty computation.

Autonomy and Accountability: As LLMs become more autonomous, questions arise about who should be held accountable for their decisions and actions. Establishing clear guidelines for responsible AI use and defining legal and ethical frameworks for accountability are essential steps in addressing this dilemma.

Impact on Employment: The widespread adoption of LLMs in various industries may lead to job displacement or changes in workforce dynamics. Mitigating the impact on employment involves reskilling and upskilling programs, as well as exploring new roles and opportunities created by AI technologies.

Dual-Use Dilemma: LLMs can be used for both beneficial and harmful purposes, such as creating persuasive misinformation or conducting automated social engineering attacks. Developing policies and regulations that restrict harmful uses while promoting beneficial applications is crucial in addressing this dilemma.

Strategies to Address Ethical Challenges

To effectively address the ethical challenges associated with LLMs, several strategies can be implemented:

Ethics by Design: Incorporating ethical considerations into the design and development process of LLMs can help preemptively identify and mitigate potential ethical issues.

Interdisciplinary Collaboration: Engaging experts from diverse disciplines including ethics, law, sociology, and computer science can provide comprehensive perspectives on the ethical implications of LLMs.

Public Engagement and Education: Educating the public about the capabilities and limitations of LLMs, as well as fostering discussions about ethical concerns, can promote awareness and informed decision-making.

Regulatory Frameworks: Developing regulatory frameworks that govern the responsible development and deployment of LLMs can ensure compliance with ethical standards and protect societal interests.

Ethical Audits and Impact Assessments: Conducting regular ethical audits and impact assessments of LLMs can identify ethical risks and guide the implementation of mitigation strategies.

Continuous Monitoring and Feedback: Implementing mechanisms for continuous monitoring and gathering feedback from stakeholders can facilitate adaptive responses to emerging ethical challenges.

While LLMs offer unprecedented opportunities for innovation and advancement, their ethical use requires careful consideration of guidelines, proactive mitigation of ethical dilemmas, and the implementation of strategies to address these challenges. By prioritizing transparency, accountability, fairness, and user empowerment, stakeholders can harness the transformative potential of LLMs while minimizing potential harms to individuals and society. Ethical stewardship of LLMs is not merely a technical imperative but a moral obligation to ensure that AI technologies contribute positively to the well-being of humanity.

Chapter 30 Technical Challenges

The computing faces numerous intricate challenges. These challenges not only shape the development of new technologies but also dictate the efficiency and sustainability of existing systems. Among the foremost technical hurdles are computational limitations, energy consumption concerns, memory management issues, and the drive towards enhanced efficiency. This exploration delves into these critical areas, examining their impacts, ongoing research efforts, and potential future directions.

Computational Limitations

Computational limitations refer to the barriers that restrict the processing power and speed of computing systems.

Despite exponential growth in computing power over the past decades, certain fundamental constraints persist.

Moore's Law and Beyond

Moore's Law, the observation that the number of transistors on a microchip doubles approximately every two years, has been the driving force behind the increase in computational power. However, as transistor sizes approach physical limits and heat dissipation becomes more challenging, this trend is slowing down. The industry is exploring alternative technologies such as quantum computing and neuromorphic computing to push beyond the boundaries of traditional silicon-based systems.

Parallelization and Scalability

Another facet of computational limitations lies in the effective utilization of parallel processing. While modern

CPUs and GPUs leverage parallel architectures, not all algorithms can be easily parallelized. This disparity leads to inefficiencies and bottlenecks, especially in tasks where sequential processing is unavoidable.

Real-time and Complex Simulations

For applications requiring real-time responses or complex simulations (such as weather forecasting or molecular dynamics), computational limitations pose significant challenges. These tasks demand enormous computational resources, pushing the boundaries of existing hardware capabilities.

Energy Consumption

Energy consumption has emerged as a critical concern in computing, driven by both environmental sustainability goals and practical limitations in power infrastructure.

Power Efficiency in Devices

The proliferation of mobile devices and IoT (Internet of

Things) has heightened the demand for energy-efficient computing. Low-power processors and advanced power management techniques are essential to prolonging battery life and reducing environmental impact.

Data Centers and Cloud Computing

Data centers, which underpin cloud computing services, are notorious for their high energy consumption. Cooling systems alone can consume a substantial portion of a data center's power budget. Innovations in server design, energy-efficient cooling technologies, and renewable energy integration are crucial for reducing the environmental footprint of these facilities.

Edge Computing and Energy Constraints

Edge computing, which involves processing data closer to the source of generation (at the edge of the network), aims to reduce latency and bandwidth usage. However, edge devices often operate under stringent energy constraints, necessitating lightweight algorithms and efficient hardware designs.

Memory and Efficiency Issues

Memory management and efficiency are perennial challenges in computing, influencing system responsiveness, scalability, and cost-effectiveness.

Memory Hierarchy and Access Speeds

Modern computing systems employ a hierarchy of memory types, ranging from high-speed registers and caches to slower but higher-capacity main memory and storage. Efficient management of this hierarchy is crucial for optimizing performance and minimizing latency.

Memory Leaks and Resource Management

Memory leaks, where a program fails to release memory after use, can lead to performance degradation and system crashes. Effective memory management techniques, such as garbage collection and smart allocation strategies, are essential for maintaining system stability and efficiency.

Big Data and Storage Solutions

The advent of big data has underscored the need for scalable and cost-effective storage solutions. Traditional storage technologies, such as hard disk drives (HDDs) and solid-state drives (SSDs), continue to evolve to meet the demands of data-intensive applications while balancing cost and performance considerations.

Innovations and Future Directions

In addressing these challenges, researchers and industry leaders are exploring a variety of innovative approaches and technologies.

Quantum Computing

Quantum computing holds promise for solving complex problems that are intractable for classical computers. Despite current technical limitations, ongoing research aims to harness quantum phenomena to revolutionize fields such as cryptography, optimization, and materials science.

Neuromorphic Computing

Inspired by the human brain, neuromorphic computing seeks to build systems that mimic the brain's neural networks. These systems promise efficient processing of sensory data and adaptive learning capabilities, paving the way for advanced AI applications and autonomous systems.

Advances in AI and Machine Learning

AI and machine learning algorithms are driving innovations in computational efficiency. Techniques such as deep learning have achieved remarkable results in tasks such as image recognition and natural language processing, albeit at the cost of intensive computational resources. Continued research focuses on developing more efficient algorithms and hardware accelerators tailored for specific AI workloads.

Sustainable Computing Practices

Efforts towards sustainability include designing energy-efficient hardware, optimizing software for minimal power consumption, and promoting renewable energy use in data centers. Initiatives like the Green Grid consortium and the development of energy-efficient computing standards aim to mitigate the environmental impact of computing infrastructure.

The technical challenges facing computing—computational limitations, energy consumption, memory issues, and efficiency—are multifaceted and interlinked. Addressing these challenges requires collaborative efforts across disciplines, from materials science and physics to computer architecture and software engineering. As researchers and engineers continue to push the boundaries of what's possible, the evolution of computing systems holds promise for transformative advancements in technology, science, and society at large. By innovating responsibly and sustainably, we can unlock new opportunities while safeguarding our planet's resources for future generations.

Chapter 31 Regulatory Considerations

In recent years, Language Models (LMs) and specifically Large Language Models (LLMs) have emerged as powerful tools in natural language processing, transforming various industries and applications. However, their rapid development has raised significant regulatory and legal considerations. This essay explores the current regulatory landscape impacting LLMs, potential future legal frameworks, and the implications for stakeholders.

Current Regulations Impacting LLMs

As of the latest updates, the regulatory environment surrounding LLMs is still evolving and varies significantly across jurisdictions. The primary regulatory concerns can be categorized into several key areas:

Data Privacy and Protection:

LLMs rely heavily on vast amounts of data for training, which often includes personal information. Regulations such as the European Union's General Data Protection Regulation (GDPR) and the California Consumer Privacy Act (CCPA) impose strict requirements on the collection, storage, and processing of personal data. Compliance with these regulations is crucial for LLM developers and users to avoid penalties and maintain trust.

Bias and Fairness:

LLMs have been criticized for perpetuating biases present in their training data, leading to discriminatory outcomes. Regulators are increasingly focusing on ensuring fairness and transparency in AI systems, including LLMs. Guidelines such as the AI Act in the EU and similar initiatives globally aim to address these issues by promoting ethical AI development practices.

Intellectual Property (IP) Rights:

The output generated by LLMs, such as texts, images, and code, raises questions about ownership and copyright. Existing IP laws may not adequately address the novel challenges posed by AI-generated content. Clarification is needed regarding whether AI systems can create copyrightable works and who owns the rights to such creations.

Security and Accountability:

LLMs can potentially be exploited for malicious purposes, including spreading misinformation or conducting cyber-attacks. Regulators are exploring ways to enhance the security of AI systems and hold developers accountable for any harm caused by their creations. Standards for robustness, safety, and accountability are being developed to mitigate these risks.

Regulatory Oversight and Certification:

There is a growing call for regulatory bodies to establish clear guidelines and certification processes for LLMs. This includes assessing the reliability, safety, and ethical implications of deploying LLMs in various sectors such as healthcare, finance, and legal services.

International Coordination:

LLMs operate across borders, posing challenges for regulatory harmonization. Efforts are underway to establish international standards and frameworks that facilitate the global deployment of LLMs while ensuring consistency in regulatory requirements.

Potential Future Legal Frameworks

Looking ahead, the future legal frameworks for LLMs are likely to be shaped by ongoing developments in technology, policy, and societal expectations. Several key trends and potential legal considerations include:

Enhanced Data Governance:

Future regulations may impose stricter requirements for data governance, including enhanced transparency about data sources used to train LLMs. This could involve mandates for data provenance and quality assurance to mitigate biases and ensure fairness.

Algorithmic Accountability:

There is a growing demand for accountability in AI systems, including LLMs. Future legal frameworks may require developers to provide explanations for AI-generated decisions and outcomes, particularly in high-stakes applications like healthcare and criminal justice.

Ethical AI Standards:

Ethical guidelines and standards for AI development are likely to become formalized into regulatory requirements. Principles such as transparency, fairness, accountability, and human oversight may be enshrined in law to guide the design, deployment, and use of LLMs.

Sector-Specific Regulations:

Different sectors may develop tailored regulations for the use of LLMs based on their specific risks and societal impacts. For instance, healthcare regulators may focus on patient safety and data privacy, while financial regulators may emphasize market integrity and consumer protection.

International Cooperation:

Harmonization efforts across jurisdictions will be critical to facilitate the global adoption of LLMs. International agreements and frameworks may emerge to promote interoperability and mutual recognition of regulatory standards while respecting cultural and legal differences.

Innovation and Competition:

Legal frameworks should balance fostering innovation in LLM technology with ensuring fair competition and preventing monopolistic practices. Antitrust laws may need to adapt to address concerns related to AI dominance and market concentration.

Public Engagement and Oversight:

Increasing public awareness and engagement in AI governance will influence future legal frameworks. Mechanisms for public consultation, stakeholder engagement,

361

and democratic oversight of AI policy decisions may be formalized to ensure inclusivity and legitimacy.

Implications for Stakeholders

The evolving regulatory and legal landscape for LLMs will have profound implications for various stakeholders:

- Developers and Researchers: They will need to navigate complex regulatory requirements, invest in compliance measures, and adopt ethical AI practices to mitigate legal risks and maintain public trust.

- Businesses and Industries: Companies leveraging LLMs must ensure compliance with sector-specific regulations, manage risks related to data privacy and bias, and anticipate regulatory changes that could impact their operations.

- Governments and Regulators: Regulatory bodies face the challenge of balancing innovation with risk management, requiring collaboration with stakeholders to develop effective and enforceable legal frameworks.

- Civil Society and Consumers: Advocacy groups and consumers will advocate for transparency, accountability, and ethical use of LLMs, influencing regulatory priorities and shaping public discourse on AI governance.

While LLMs offer transformative potential across various domains, their development and deployment are accompanied by significant regulatory and legal considerations. Current regulations focus on data privacy, bias mitigation, and accountability, while future legal frameworks are expected to evolve to address emerging challenges and societal expectations. Collaboration among stakeholders and international cooperation will be essential to develop robust and ethical AI governance frameworks that promote innovation while protecting rights and values in the AI era.

Chapter 32 Future of LLMs

In recent years, Language Models (LMs) have undergone a revolutionary transformation, moving from mere text generators to sophisticated systems capable of understanding, reasoning, and even holding contextual conversations. This evolution has significantly impacted various fields, including natural language processing, artificial intelligence, and human-computer interaction. Looking ahead, the future of LMs promises even more profound advancements, driven by emerging trends and technologies that are poised to reshape our interactions with digital assistants, customer service bots, content generation tools, and beyond.

Emerging Trends in LLMs

Multimodal Capabilities: Current LLMs primarily process and generate text. However, future advancements will integrate multimodal capabilities, enabling models to understand and generate text, images, and possibly videos seamlessly. This will enhance their utility in fields like multimedia content creation, virtual reality environments, and personalized user experiences.

Contextual Understanding: Future LLMs will further refine their ability to understand context in conversations and tasks. This includes improved sentiment analysis, nuanced responses based on user history, and more sophisticated dialogue management systems. Such capabilities are crucial for applications in customer service, virtual assistants, and educational tools.

Ethical and Responsible AI: As LLMs become more pervasive in everyday life, concerns around ethics, bias, and misuse become increasingly pertinent. Future developments will likely focus on designing LLMs with robust ethical guidelines, transparency in decision-making processes, and mechanisms to mitigate biases in training data.

Personalization and Adaptation: LLMs of the future will evolve to become more personalized, adapting responses and interactions based on individual user preferences, behavior patterns, and specific contexts. This personalization will enhance user satisfaction and utility across various domains.

Domain-Specific LLMs: While current LLMs are general-purpose, future trends suggest a move towards specialized or domain-specific models. These LLMs will be tailored for specific industries such as healthcare, finance, legal services (LLMs for law), where nuanced understanding of domain-specific jargon and regulations is crucial.

Enhanced User Interfaces: The interface through which users interact with LLMs is also evolving. Future LLMs may integrate with augmented reality (AR) or virtual reality (VR) environments, enabling more immersive and intuitive interactions. This could revolutionize fields like gaming, virtual education, and remote collaboration.

Predictions for the Next Decade

Advancements in Generative Models: The next decade will witness significant advancements in generative models, leading to LLMs that not only understand but can also generate highly coherent and contextually appropriate content across multiple modalities.

Broader Deployment Across Industries: LLMs will increasingly find applications in diverse sectors such as healthcare (medical diagnosis support), education (personalized tutoring), finance (automated customer service), and entertainment (content creation). This widespread adoption will drive innovation and specialization in LLM technology.

Integration with IoT and Edge Computing: As Internet of

Things (IoT) devices become ubiquitous, LLMs will integrate with edge computing networks to provide real-time, personalized responses directly on devices like smart speakers, wearable, and autonomous vehicles.

Breakthroughs in Language Understanding: Breakthroughs in natural language understanding (NLU) will enable LLMs to comprehend and generate nuanced human-like responses, making them more adept at handling complex queries and fostering deeper interactions.

Regulatory Frameworks and Ethical Guidelines: Governments and tech companies will collaborate to establish regulatory frameworks and ethical guidelines for the development and deployment of LLMs. This will ensure transparency, accountability, and fairness in their use across different sectors.

Global Accessibility and Language Support: Future LLMs will offer broader language support and accessibility features, empowering users from diverse linguistic backgrounds to benefit from advanced AI-driven interactions and services.

 Collaboration with Human Experts: LLMs will increasingly collaborate with human experts in fields such as medicine, law, and research, providing valuable insights, automating routine tasks, and augmenting human decision-making processes.

The future of Language Models is poised for unprecedented growth and innovation, driven by emerging trends in multimodal capabilities, contextual understanding, ethical considerations, and personalized interactions. Over the next decade, we can expect LLMs to become more integrated into our daily lives, transforming industries, enhancing user experiences, and shaping the way we interact with information and technology. However, as with any transformative technology, careful consideration of ethical implications and regulatory frameworks will be essential to ensure that LLMs contribute positively to society while mitigating potential risks. As researchers, developers, and policymakers continue to collaborate, the potential of LLMs to revolutionize communication and problem-solving across the globe remains both exciting and promising.

Chapter 33 Case Study: OpenAI's GPT Models

To provide a detailed look at the development and impact of GPT-2, GPT-3, and GPT-4, we need to delve into the evolution of these models, their technological advancements, applications across various domains, and their implications for society.

Introduction to Generative Pre-trained Transformers (GPT)

Generative Pre-trained Transformers, developed by OpenAI, represent a significant leap in natural language processing (NLP) technology. These models are based on the Transformer architecture, known for its ability to handle sequential data efficiently. The key innovation in GPT models lies in their pre-training on vast amounts of text data, followed by fine-tuning on specific tasks, enabling them to generate human-like text and perform a range of NLP tasks with high accuracy.

GPT-2: Emergence and Initial Impact

Development

GPT-2 was introduced in February 2019, marking a major milestone in AI and NLP research. It was trained on 40GB of internet text data, encompassing a wide array of topics and writing styles. GPT-2 featured 1.5 billion parameters, making it one of the largest and most powerful language models at the time of its release.

Impact

Text Generation: GPT-2 demonstrated remarkable capabilities in generating coherent and contextually relevant text. Its outputs often seemed indistinguishable from human writing, sparking both fascination and concerns over the potential misuse of such technology.

Applications: Beyond text generation, GPT-2 excelled in tasks such as translation, summarization, and question-answering. It became a versatile tool for various NLP applications, empowering developers and researchers across industries.

Ethical Concerns: The release of GPT-2 also raised ethical considerations regarding the potential misuse of AI-generated content, including misinformation, propaganda, and fake news dissemination.

GPT-3: Advancements and Broader Applications

Development

GPT-3, unveiled in June 2020, represented a significant leap forward in both scale and performance compared to its predecessor. With 175 billion parameters, GPT-3 dwarfed GPT-2 in size and complexity, enabling it to handle even more sophisticated language tasks.

Impact

Performance Improvements: GPT-3 demonstrated superior performance across a wide range of benchmarks, showcasing its ability to understand and generate human-like text with unprecedented accuracy.

Scaling Effects: The sheer scale of GPT-3 allowed it to capture nuances in language and context more effectively, making it a preferred choice for complex NLP tasks such as context-aware chatbots and content generation.

Applications in Industry: GPT-3 found applications in diverse fields, including customer service automation, content creation, educational tools, and even creative writing. Its versatility and high performance made it a sought-after technology in both research and commercial sectors.

Ethical and Societal Implications: As with GPT-2, GPT-3 raised concerns about ethical use, algorithmic biases, and the potential societal impact of AI technologies becoming more ubiquitous and powerful.

GPT-4: Cutting-Edge Innovations and Future Directions

Development

While specific details about GPT-4 are not yet publicly available (as of the time of this writing), it is expected to build upon the successes of its predecessors. Anticipated advancements may include even larger model sizes, improved contextual understanding, and enhanced capabilities in multimodal tasks (integrating text with images or other data types).

Potential Impact

Technological Advancements: GPT-4 could push the boundaries of what is possible in NLP, potentially offering more nuanced understanding of language, improved coherence in text generation, and better integration with other AI modalities.

Applications: Future applications of GPT-4 may span across fields such as healthcare (medical diagnosis and personalized treatment recommendations), finance (algorithmic trading and risk assessment), and creative industries (artistic content generation).

 Ethical Considerations: As AI technologies evolve, ongoing discussions about responsible AI development, transparency in AI systems, and mitigation of potential harms will remain critical.

The development and impact of GPT-2, GPT-3, and the anticipated GPT-4 illustrate the rapid evolution of AI and NLP technologies. These models have not only pushed the boundaries of what AI can achieve in language understanding and generation but also sparked important conversations about ethics, regulation, and the future societal implications of AI. As we move forward, balancing technological advancements with ethical considerations will be crucial in harnessing the full potential of these transformative technologies for the benefit of humanity.

Chapter 34 Case Study: BERT and Its Variants

In recent years, advancements in natural language processing (NLP) have been propelled by the development and refinement of deep learning models, particularly transformer-based architectures like BERT (Bidirectional Encoder Representations from Transformers). BERT, and its subsequent variants, have significantly influenced the landscape of NLP, revolutionizing tasks such as language understanding, generation, and translation. This case study delves into the application and influence of BERT in NLP, exploring its evolution, impact across various domains, and ongoing research trends.

Evolution of BERT

BERT, introduced by Devlin et al. in 2018, marked a pivotal moment in NLP by demonstrating state-of-the-art results across a range of language understanding tasks. Unlike earlier models that processed text in a unidirectional manner, BERT leveraged the transformer architecture's bidirectional nature to capture contextual information more effectively. This bidirectionality allowed BERT to learn deep, context-rich representations of words and sentences, essential for tasks like sentiment analysis, question answering, and named entity recognition.

The key innovation of BERT lies in its pre-training and fine-tuning strategy. Pre-training involves unsupervised learning on large corpora of text, where BERT learns to predict masked words within sentences and understand sentence relationships through tasks like next sentence prediction.

Fine-tuning adapts BERT's pre-trained weights to specific downstream tasks with comparatively smaller labeled datasets, achieving high performance with minimal task-specific training.

Applications of BERT in NLP

1. Sentiment Analysis and Classification

BERT's ability to grasp nuanced contextual meanings has made it particularly effective in sentiment analysis. By fine-tuning on sentiment-labeled datasets, BERT models can accurately discern the sentiment expressed in text across various domains such as product reviews, social media posts, and customer feedback.

2. Question Answering

BERT has excelled in question answering tasks, where it

reads a passage of text and identifies the most relevant answer to a given question. This capability has practical applications in chatbots, search engines, and customer support systems, enhancing the accuracy and efficiency of information retrieval processes.

3. Named Entity Recognition (NER)

NER involves identifying and classifying entities mentioned in text, such as names of people, organizations, or locations. BERT's contextual understanding enables more accurate recognition of named entities, crucial for information extraction tasks in fields like biomedical research, news analysis, and legal document processing.

4. Machine Translation

Although traditionally dominated by sequence-to-sequence models, BERT and its variants have contributed to improving machine translation by providing better contextual embeddings. Integrating BERT into translation models enhances their ability to capture subtle nuances in meaning and context, improving the fidelity of translated text.

5. Text Summarization

BERT has also been applied to abstractive text summarization, where it generates concise summaries that capture the essential information from longer documents. By understanding the context and relationships between sentences, BERT-based models produce summaries that are coherent and informative.

Influence of BERT in Industry and Academia

The introduction of BERT has had profound implications for both industry and academia. In industry, many companies have adopted BERT-based models to improve the performance of their NLP applications. For instance, Google integrated BERT into its search algorithm to better understand user queries and provide more relevant search results. Similarly, social media platforms use BERT to analyze and categorize user-generated content, enhancing content moderation and recommendation systems.

In academia, BERT has sparked a wave of research exploring its limitations, improvements, and extensions. Researchers have developed numerous variants and adaptations of BERT to address specific challenges or improve performance on particular tasks. These variants include models like RoBERTa (Robustly optimized BERT approach), ALBERT (A Lite BERT), and DistilBERT, each offering enhancements in speed, efficiency, or generalizability.

Ongoing Research and Future Directions

Despite its successes, BERT and its variants are not without limitations. The computational cost of training large transformer models remains a barrier for many researchers and organizations. Additionally, BERT's reliance on fixed-length input limits its applicability to longer documents or sequences.

Future research is focusing on overcoming these challenges and pushing the boundaries of transformer-based models in NLP. One direction involves exploring methods to enhance the interpretability of BERT embeddings, making it easier to understand how the model arrives at its decisions. Another area of interest is adapting BERT for multilingual and low-resource languages, where data scarcity poses significant challenges.

Moreover, ongoing efforts in model compression and optimization aim to make BERT more accessible for deployment on edge devices or in environments with limited computational resources. Techniques such as knowledge distillation and pruning help reduce the size of BERT models without sacrificing performance, making them more practical for real-world applications.

BERT and its variants have transformed the field of NLP,

setting new benchmarks for language understanding and representation learning. From sentiment analysis to machine translation, these models have demonstrated remarkable versatility and effectiveness across a wide range of tasks. Their impact extends beyond academia, shaping the capabilities of modern NLP systems and driving innovation in industries reliant on language processing technologies. As research continues to evolve, BERT and its successors are expected to play a pivotal role in advancing the state-of-the-art in NLP, making language-driven AI applications more accurate, efficient, and accessible than ever before. By understanding and harnessing the power of BERT, researchers and practitioners are poised to unlock new possibilities in communication, automation, and knowledge discovery through natural language understanding.

Chapter 35 Case Study: Commercial Applications

In recent years, the integration of Large Language Models (LLMs) into commercial applications has revolutionized various industries. LLMs, powered by advanced artificial intelligence techniques such as deep learning, natural language processing (NLP), and transformer architectures, have demonstrated remarkable capabilities in understanding and generating human-like text. This case study explores several examples of how companies are leveraging LLMs to enhance their products and services across different sectors.

Natural Language Understanding in Customer Service:

One of the most prominent applications of LLMs is in improving natural language understanding (NLU) for customer service interactions. Companies like Zendesk have integrated LLMs into their customer support platforms to automate responses, understand complex queries, and provide personalized solutions in real-time. By training these models on vast amounts of historical customer data, Zendesk's system can now handle a wide range of inquiries with minimal human intervention, thereby improving efficiency and customer satisfaction.

Content Generation and Personalization:

The Washington Post is a notable example of a media company using LLMs to enhance content generation and personalization. By deploying LLMs like GPT-3, The Washington Post has been able to automate routine reporting tasks such as summarizing articles, generating headlines, and even drafting initial versions of stories based on raw data inputs. This not only speeds up the news production process but also allows journalists to focus more on investigative reporting and in-depth analysis.

Virtual Assistants and Smart Devices:

Companies like Amazon with their Alexa virtual assistant and Google with Google Assistant have integrated LLMs to improve the conversational abilities and overall intelligence of their smart devices. These assistants rely on LLMs to understand user queries, execute tasks like setting reminders or ordering products online, and even engage in more natural, human-like conversations. The continuous improvement in language understanding and generation capabilities of these assistants showcases the evolving applications of LLMs in everyday consumer technology.

Financial Services and Risk Management:

In the financial sector, companies such as JP Morgan Chase have adopted LLMs to analyze vast amounts of textual data from financial reports, news articles, and social media to assess market sentiment, predict economic trends, and manage investment portfolios more effectively. By leveraging the natural language processing capabilities of LLMs, JP Morgan Chase can extract actionable insights from unstructured data sources, providing their clients with timely and informed decision-making support.

Healthcare and Medical Text Analysis:

IBM Watson Health exemplifies the use of LLMs in

healthcare by employing advanced NLP techniques to analyze medical literature, patient records, and clinical trial data. Watson Health's LLM-powered systems assist healthcare professionals in diagnosing illnesses, recommending treatment plans based on the latest research, and even predicting patient outcomes with greater accuracy. This application not only improves the efficiency of medical professionals but also enhances patient care by integrating cutting-edge AI technologies into clinical practice.

E-commerce and Recommendation Systems:

Companies like Netflix and Amazon utilize LLMs to enhance their recommendation systems, which suggest products, movies, or shows based on user preferences and behavior patterns. By analyzing historical user data, these systems can predict user interests and preferences more accurately, thereby improving customer engagement and driving sales. LLM-powered recommendation engines are instrumental in personalizing the online shopping and entertainment experiences of millions of users worldwide.

Legal and Regulatory Compliance:

In the legal sector, firms such as Luminance use LLMs to streamline contract review processes and ensure regulatory compliance. These LLM-powered platforms can quickly analyze complex legal documents, identify potential risks, and extract key clauses with high accuracy. By automating labor-intensive tasks traditionally performed by lawyers, Luminance and similar companies enable legal professionals to focus on higher-value activities, thereby increasing productivity and reducing operational costs.

Education and Language Learning:

Companies like Duolingo have integrated LLMs into their language learning platforms to provide personalized tutoring and feedback to millions of users worldwide. By analyzing user responses and interactions, Duolingo's LLM-powered systems can adapt lesson plans in real-time, identify areas where learners may need additional practice, and simulate natural conversations to improve language fluency. This application demonstrates how LLMs can enhance educational experiences by providing tailored learning experiences that cater to individual needs and learning styles.

Future Directions and Challenges:

While the commercial applications of LLMs have brought about significant advancements across various industries, several challenges remain. Issues such as data privacy concerns, bias in AI models, and the ethical implications of deploying LLMs in decision-making processes require careful consideration. Furthermore, the rapid pace of technological innovation necessitates ongoing research and development to address these challenges and unlock the full potential of LLMs in a responsible and ethical manner.

The integration of Large Language Models into commercial applications represents a paradigm shift in how businesses leverage artificial intelligence to enhance productivity, improve customer experiences, and drive innovation across diverse sectors. As companies continue to innovate and adapt to the capabilities of LLMs, the future promises even more transformative applications that could reshape industries and society as a whole.

Chapter 36 Setting Up the Environment

In modern software development and data science, setting up the right environment is crucial for efficiency, collaboration, and scalability. Whether you're a developer, a data scientist, or an IT professional, the choices you make in terms of tools, libraries, and deployment methods can significantly impact your productivity and the success of your projects. This article explores the essentials of setting up an environment, focusing on necessary tools and libraries, as well as the decision between cloud and local deployment options.

Necessary Tools and Libraries

The choice of tools and libraries depends largely on the specific requirements of your project, but there are some fundamental components that are commonly used across various domains.

Integrated Development Environments (IDEs)

An IDE is a crucial tool for software developers as it provides a comprehensive environment to write, test, and debug code efficiently. Popular IDEs include:

Visual Studio Code (VS Code): Known for its lightweight yet powerful features, extensibility through plugins, and support for a wide range of programming languages.

PyCharm: Specifically designed for Python development, PyCharm offers advanced features like code analysis, debugging, and integration with popular frameworks like Django and Flask.

IntelliJ IDEA: Ideal for Java developers, IntelliJ IDEA provides smart code assistance, deep code understanding, and integration with build tools like Maven and Gradle.

Eclipse: Widely used for Java development, Eclipse is known

for its extensibility and support for a wide range of plugins.

Jupyter Notebooks / JupyterLab: Essential for data scientists, Jupyter provides an interactive environment for data exploration, visualization, and machine learning model prototyping.

Version Control Systems

Effective version control is crucial for managing changes to codebases and collaborating with team members. Git is the most widely used version control system, often coupled with platforms like GitHub, GitLab, or Bitbucket for hosting repositories and enabling collaboration.

Package Management

Depending on the programming language, package managers simplify the process of installing, updating, and managing dependencies. Examples include npm (for Node.js), pip (for Python), Maven (for Java), and RubyGems (for Ruby).

Virtual Environments

Virtual environments enable developers to create isolated environments for different projects, ensuring dependencies are managed separately. Tools like virtualenv (for Python) and venv (built-in with Python 3) are commonly used for this purpose.

Testing Frameworks

To ensure code quality and reliability, testing frameworks such as JUnit (for Java), pytest (for Python), Jasmine (for JavaScript), and RSpec (for Ruby) are employed, depending on the programming language and application type.

Database Management Systems (DBMS)

For applications involving data storage, selecting the right DBMS is crucial. Options range from relational databases like MySQL, PostgreSQL, and SQLite to NoSQL databases such as MongoDB and Redis, each suited to different use cases based on scalability, performance, and data structure requirements.

Cloud vs Local Deployment

The choice between deploying your applications and environments in the cloud or locally depends on several factors, including scalability needs, cost considerations, security requirements, and development team preferences.

Cloud Deployment

Scalability: Cloud platforms like Amazon Web Services (AWS), Microsoft Azure, and Google Cloud Platform (GCP) offer scalable resources that can expand or contract based on demand, making them ideal for applications with unpredictable traffic patterns.

Cost Efficiency: While cloud services generally involve a recurring cost, they eliminate the need for upfront hardware investment and provide cost-effective scaling options.

Flexibility and Accessibility: Cloud services enable teams to collaborate easily regardless of geographic location, with access to resources from anywhere with an internet connection.

Managed Services: Cloud providers offer managed services for databases, caching, container orchestration (e.g., Kubernetes), and other infrastructure components, reducing the operational burden on development teams.

Security: Cloud providers invest heavily in security measures, often offering robust encryption, compliance certifications, and advanced threat detection systems.

Local Deployment

Control: Deploying locally gives developers full control over the environment, including hardware specifications, software configurations, and network setup.

Cost: Initial setup costs for local deployment can be higher due to the need to purchase hardware and software licenses, although ongoing operational costs might be lower.

Performance:

In some cases, local deployments can offer better performance, especially for applications that require low latency or involve large volumes of data processing.

Data Privacy:

Organizations with strict data privacy regulations or concerns may prefer to keep sensitive data on-premises to maintain full control over security measures.

Development and Testing: Local environments are often preferred for development and testing stages, allowing developers to iterate quickly without relying on external internet connectivity or cloud infrastructure.

Setting up the environment for software development or data

science involves selecting the right tools, libraries, and deployment strategies tailored to the specific needs of your project.

Whether you opt for cloud-based solutions for scalability and flexibility or prefer the control and customization of local deployments, each approach has its advantages and considerations.

By leveraging the appropriate IDEs, version control systems, package managers, testing frameworks, and database management systems, developers can streamline development workflows and ensure code quality.

Similarly, choosing between cloud and local deployment options requires careful consideration of factors like scalability, cost, security, and performance to align with project requirements and organizational goals.

Ultimately, a well-planned environment setup enhances productivity, fosters collaboration, and contributes to the overall success of software projects, empowering teams to deliver high-quality solutions efficiently and effectively in today's competitive landscape.

Chapter 37 Building a Simple Language Model

In recent years, language models have become increasingly prevalent in various applications, from virtual assistants to text generation systems. These models are designed to understand and generate human-like text based on patterns and structures learned from vast amounts of data. Building a simple language model (LLM) can be an exciting introduction to this field, offering insights into natural language processing (NLP) and machine learning techniques. In this guide, we will walk through the process of creating a basic language model using Python and the TensorFlow library.

Understanding Language Models

Before diving into the technical details, let's clarify what a language model is and what it aims to achieve. A language model is a probabilistic model that predicts the likelihood of a sequence of words occurring in a given context. It learns from a corpus of text data, capturing patterns in language such as grammar, semantics, and syntax. The model's ability to generate coherent text stems from its understanding of these linguistic structures.

Step 1: Choose a Dataset

The first step in building a language model is selecting an appropriate dataset. The quality and size of your dataset significantly influence the performance and capabilities of your model. For our simple language model, we can start with a small corpus such as movie reviews, news headlines, or even text from classic literature. For this example, let's use a dataset of movie reviews from the IMDb dataset.

Step 2: Preprocess the Data

Once you have your dataset, preprocessing is necessary to prepare the text for model training. This step involves:

- Tokenization: Breaking down text into individual words or subword units (tokens).

- Normalization: Converting text to lowercase, removing punctuation, and handling special characters.

- Vectorization: Representing words numerically (e.g., using one-hot encoding or word embeddings like Word2Vec or GloVe).

In Python, libraries like NLTK (Natural Language Toolkit)

and TensorFlow can assist in these tasks, making data preparation more manageable.

Step 3: Build the Language Model

Now, we can proceed to construct our language model using TensorFlow. TensorFlow provides a powerful framework for building neural networks, including recurrent neural networks (RNNs) and more advanced architectures like long short-term memory networks (LSTMs) or transformers. For simplicity, we'll start with a basic LSTM-based model.

Example Code Snippet (using TensorFlow/Keras):

```python
import tensorflow as tf
```

```python
from tensorflow.keras.layers import
Embedding, LSTM, Dense
from tensorflow.keras.models import
Sequential

# Define model architecture
model = Sequential()
model.add(Embedding(input_dim=vocab_siz
e, output_dim=embedding_dim,
input_length=max_seq_length))
model.add(LSTM(units=128))
model.add(Dense(units=vocab_size,
activation='softmax'))

# Compile model
model.compile(optimizer='adam',
loss='categorical_crossentropy',
```

```
metrics=['accuracy'])


 Train model
model.fit(X_train, y_train, epochs=10,
batch_size=32)
 ` ` `
```

Step 4: Train and Evaluate the Model

After defining the model architecture, the next step is training. Training involves feeding the preprocessed data into the model and adjusting the model's weights based on the error (loss) calculated during training. For language models, the evaluation often includes metrics such as perplexity or accuracy, measuring how well the model predicts the next word in a sequence.

Step 5: Generate Text

Once the model is trained and evaluated, you can use it to generate text based on a seed input. This process involves predicting the next word given a sequence of words from the dataset. By sampling from the predicted probabilities (using techniques like softmax), the model generates text that follows the patterns it has learned.

Step 6: Fine-tuning and Optimization

Building a simple language model is just the beginning. To improve performance, consider:

- Hyperparameter tuning: Adjusting parameters like learning rate, batch size, and model architecture.
- Data augmentation: Adding more diverse data or preprocessing techniques.

- Model evaluation: Testing the model on different datasets or real-world scenarios.

Building a simple language model involves understanding the fundamentals of natural language processing, data preprocessing, model architecture, and training.

With frameworks like TensorFlow and Python's rich ecosystem of libraries, creating and experimenting with language models has become more accessible than ever.

Whether for educational purposes or practical applications, the ability to generate text using machine learning models opens doors to a wide range of possibilities in AI and NLP.

By following the steps outlined in this guide, you can embark on your journey to creating and exploring the fascinating world of language models. As you gain more experience, you can delve deeper into advanced techniques and applications,

contributing to the evolving landscape of artificial intelligence

and machine learning.

Chapter 38 Optimizing Performance

In machine learning and artificial intelligence, optimizing performance is a critical endeavor. Whether you're dealing with training complex neural networks or deploying models in real-time applications, achieving high performance and efficiency is paramount. This article explores various techniques and strategies used to enhance model performance and efficiency, focusing on both theoretical approaches and practical implementations.

Understanding Performance Optimization

Performance optimization in machine learning refers to the

process of improving the accuracy, speed, scalability, and resource utilization of models. It involves a combination of algorithmic improvements, parameter tuning, and hardware/software optimizations. The goals typically include reducing training time, improving inference speed, minimizing resource consumption, and enhancing overall model effectiveness.

Techniques for Improving Model Performance

Feature Engineering

Feature engineering plays a crucial role in model performance. By selecting, transforming, and creating features that are most relevant to the problem at hand, one can significantly enhance the predictive power of machine learning models. Techniques such as dimensionality reduction (e.g., PCA), feature scaling, and feature selection help in extracting meaningful information and reducing noise from the data.

Hyperparameter Tuning

Hyperparameters are parameters that are set before the learning process begins. Optimizing these hyperparameters can drastically improve model performance. Techniques like grid search, random search, and Bayesian optimization are commonly used to find the optimal values for hyperparameters such as learning rate, batch size, regularization parameters, and network architecture.

Algorithm Selection

Choosing the right algorithm for a given problem can have a significant impact on performance. Different algorithms have varying strengths and weaknesses concerning accuracy, speed, and scalability. For instance, decision trees may work well with structured data, while deep learning models excel with unstructured data like images and text.

Ensemble Methods

Ensemble methods combine multiple models to improve predictive performance. Techniques like bagging (e.g., Random Forests), boosting (e.g., Gradient Boosting Machines), and stacking help in reducing bias and variance, thereby enhancing overall model accuracy. Ensemble methods are particularly effective when individual models perform differently on subsets of data or when dealing with noisy data.

Regularization

Regularization techniques such as L1 (Lasso) and L2 (Ridge) regularization help prevent overfitting by penalizing large coefficients. Regularization adds a penalty term to the loss function, encouraging the model to choose simpler parameter values. This leads to improved generalization and better performance on unseen data.

Transfer Learning

Transfer learning leverages knowledge gained from one task to improve learning in another related task. Pre-trained models, such as those trained on large datasets like ImageNet for image recognition tasks, can be fine-tuned on smaller, domain-specific datasets. This approach not only saves training time and computational resources but also improves model accuracy, especially when data is limited.

Techniques for Improving Model Efficiency

Hardware Acceleration

Utilizing specialized hardware accelerators such as GPUs (Graphics Processing Units) and TPUs (Tensor Processing Units) can significantly speed up training and inference times. These hardware platforms are optimized for parallel processing, which is well-suited for the matrix calculations involved in neural networks and other machine learning algorithms.

Quantization

Quantization involves reducing the precision of numerical representations in models. For example, converting 32-bit floating-point numbers to 8-bit integers can lead to smaller model sizes and faster computations with minimal loss in accuracy. Quantization is particularly useful for deploying models on resource-constrained devices like mobile phones and IoT devices.

Model Pruning

Model pruning involves removing unnecessary connections (weights) from a trained model. Techniques like weight pruning, unit pruning, and structured pruning aim to reduce the size of neural networks without sacrificing performance. Pruned models require fewer computations during inference, leading to faster execution times and reduced memory footprint.

Model Compression

Model compression techniques, such as knowledge distillation and parameter sharing, aim to reduce the size of complex models while retaining their performance. Knowledge distillation transfers knowledge from a larger, more accurate model (teacher) to a smaller model (student), enabling faster inference on devices with limited computational resources.

Batch Normalization and Optimizers

Batch normalization normalizes activations between layers, stabilizing the learning process and reducing the number of training iterations required to converge. Optimizers like Adam, RMSprop, and SGD with momentum help in efficiently navigating the loss landscape during training, speeding up convergence and improving overall efficiency.

Practical Considerations and Challenges

While optimizing model performance and efficiency offers

substantial benefits, several challenges must be addressed:

- Data Quality and Quantity: High-quality, representative data

is essential for training accurate models. Insufficient or biased

data can lead to poor performance and generalization.

- Computational Resources: Access to sufficient

computational resources (e.g., GPUs, cloud computing

platforms) is crucial for training large-scale models and

performing hyperparameter optimization.

- Deployment Constraints: Models optimized for training

may not always be suitable for deployment on edge devices or

in real-time applications due to resource constraints and

latency requirements.

- Ethical Considerations: Optimizing performance should

also consider ethical implications, such as fairness,

transparency, and accountability in algorithmic decision-making.

Optimizing performance in machine learning involves a multifaceted approach that combines algorithmic improvements, parameter tuning, hardware optimizations, and practical considerations. By leveraging advanced techniques such as feature engineering, hyperparameter tuning, ensemble methods, and model compression, practitioners can enhance both the accuracy and efficiency of their models. As the field continues to evolve, addressing challenges such as data quality, computational resources, and deployment constraints will be crucial in achieving sustainable advancements in machine learning performance.

In summary, the journey towards optimizing model performance and efficiency is an ongoing endeavor, driven by innovation, experimentation, and a deep understanding of both theoretical concepts and practical applications in machine learning.

Chapter 39 Deployment Strategies

In deploying Language Models (LMs) into production
environments, several strategies and practices have emerged
to ensure efficient deployment, robust performance, and
seamless integration with existing systems. This article
explores various deployment strategies, best practices, and
considerations for monitoring and maintenance of Language
Models in production settings.

Deployment Strategies

Deploying Language Models involves several strategic
decisions to optimize performance, scalability, and reliability.
Here are some key deployment strategies commonly

employed:

Containerization and Microservices:

- Containerization using platforms like Docker allows for encapsulating the Language Model and its dependencies into lightweight, portable containers. This ensures consistency across different environments from development to production.

- Microservices architecture decomposes the application into smaller, manageable services. Each service can host a specific part of the LM, enabling scalability and fault isolation.

Serverless Computing:

- Leveraging serverless platforms such as AWS Lambda or Azure Functions can be advantageous for sporadic or low-latency inference tasks. It abstracts server management, automatically scaling based on demand, and optimizing cost-efficiency.

On-premises vs. Cloud Deployment:

 - Choosing between deploying on-premises or in the cloud depends on factors like data security requirements, scalability needs, and budget constraints. Cloud deployment offers flexibility, scalability, and managed services, while on-premises deployment may provide more control over data governance and compliance.

Model Versioning and Rollout:

 - Implementing robust versioning strategies ensures that updates and improvements to the LM can be managed efficiently. Techniques like A/B testing or gradual rollout (canary deployment) help validate new models before full deployment, mitigating risks and ensuring smooth transitions.

Monitoring and Logging:

 - Effective monitoring tools such as Prometheus, Grafana,

or application-specific metrics enable real-time performance monitoring, alerting, and capacity planning. Logging helps in debugging issues and understanding LM behavior in production.

Best Practices for Deploying LLMs in Production

Deploying Large Language Models (LLMs) introduces specific challenges and considerations due to their complexity and resource-intensive nature. Here are best practices to ensure successful deployment:

Performance Optimization:

- Model Quantization: Reducing precision (e.g., from 32-bit floating-point to 16-bit) can speed up inference without significantly sacrificing accuracy.

- Model Pruning: Removing redundant weights can reduce

model size and inference time.

Security and Compliance:

- Data Encryption: Encrypting data at rest and in transit ensures privacy and compliance with data protection regulations.

- Access Control: Implementing least privilege access ensures that only authorized users and services can interact with the LM.

Scalability and Load Balancing:

- Using load balancers distributes incoming traffic across multiple instances of the LM, ensuring consistent performance during high-demand periods.

- Auto-scaling: Configuring auto-scaling policies based on metrics like CPU usage or request rates ensures resources are dynamically allocated to meet varying workloads.

Continuous Integration and Deployment (CI/CD):

- Automated Testing: Incorporate rigorous automated testing (unit tests, integration tests) into CI/CD pipelines to validate model changes before deployment.

- Deployment Automation: Automate deployment processes to reduce human error and ensure consistent deployment across environments.

Version Control and Rollback:

- Utilize version control systems (e.g., Git) to track changes to model code and configurations. This facilitates easy rollback to previous versions in case of issues.

Monitoring and Maintenance

Once deployed, continuous monitoring and proactive

maintenance are crucial to ensure optimal performance and reliability of Language Models:

Performance Monitoring:

- Monitor key performance metrics such as latency, throughput, and error rates to identify performance bottlenecks and optimize resource allocation.

Resource Utilization:

- Track CPU, memory, and GPU utilization to ensure resources are adequately provisioned and to detect anomalies or inefficiencies.

Anomaly Detection:

- Implement anomaly detection algorithms to automatically detect unusual patterns or deviations in model behavior, which may indicate issues or changes in workload.

Logging and Debugging:

- Capture detailed logs of model inference requests and responses for debugging purposes. Centralized logging helps in troubleshooting issues across distributed systems.

Security Monitoring:

- Monitor access logs and audit trails to detect unauthorized access attempts or security breaches. Implementing intrusion detection systems (IDS) can enhance security posture.

Regular Updates and Patch Management:

- Stay updated with the latest patches and security updates for dependencies, frameworks, and operating systems to mitigate vulnerabilities and ensure compliance.

Capacity Planning:

- Forecast future resource requirements based on historical data and anticipated growth to avoid performance degradation during peak usage periods.

Deploying Language Models in production environments requires careful consideration of deployment strategies, adherence to best practices, and robust monitoring and maintenance procedures. By leveraging containerization, microservices, and serverless computing, organizations can achieve scalability, flexibility, and efficiency in deploying LLMs. Continuous monitoring, performance optimization, and proactive maintenance are essential for ensuring reliable and performant LLM deployments over time. Implementing these strategies and practices enables organizations to harness the full potential of Language Models while mitigating risks and maintaining operational excellence.

Chapter 40 Final Thoughts

The 21st century has already witnessed remarkable advancements in technology, with artificial intelligence (AI) leading the charge in transforming industries, economies, and societies. Among the most groundbreaking developments is the rise of Large Language Models (LLMs), which have revolutionized natural language processing (NLP). As we progress deeper into the century, several emerging trends and predictions suggest that LLMs will continue to evolve, profoundly impacting various domains. This exploration delves into these trends, highlighting the transformative potential and the challenges that lie ahead.

Advancements in Model Architecture

One of the most significant trends in the development of LLMs is the continuous enhancement of model architecture. Models like GPT-3, GPT-4, and their successors have demonstrated unprecedented capabilities in understanding and generating human-like text. The trend towards even larger and more sophisticated models is expected to continue. These advancements will likely be driven by innovations in neural network architectures, such as the introduction of more efficient transformer models, improved attention mechanisms, and novel approaches to training and optimization.

Researchers are also exploring alternatives to the traditional transformer model. For instance, the development of sparse transformers, which reduce computational requirements while maintaining performance, and the exploration of neuromorphic computing, which mimics brain architecture, are gaining traction. These innovations could lead to the creation of LLMs that are not only more powerful but also more energy-efficient and scalable.

Integration with Multimodal Systems

Another key trend is the integration of LLMs with multimodal systems, which combine text, images, audio, and video. This integration aims to create AI systems that can understand and generate content across different modalities, enhancing their versatility and functionality. For example, models that can generate descriptive text from images or create video content based on textual descriptions are already being developed. This trend is likely to advance rapidly, leading to the creation of AI systems that can seamlessly interact with the world in a more human-like manner.

The synergy between LLMs and other modalities will also drive advancements in fields like augmented reality (AR) and virtual reality (VR), enabling more immersive and interactive experiences. For instance, AI-driven avatars and virtual assistants could become more intuitive and responsive, enhancing user engagement and interaction in virtual environments.

Customization and Personalization

As LLMs become more sophisticated, there is a growing emphasis on customization and personalization. Future LLMs are expected to be designed to better understand individual preferences, contexts, and needs. This trend is driven by advancements in techniques such as fine-tuning, few-shot learning, and transfer learning, which allow models to be tailored to specific tasks or users with minimal data.

Personalized AI systems could revolutionize various sectors, including healthcare, education, and customer service. For instance, in healthcare, LLMs could be fine-tuned to provide personalized medical advice and treatment plans based on an individual's medical history and genetic profile. In education, AI tutors could adapt their teaching methods to the learning styles and paces of individual students, enhancing educational outcomes.

Ethical and Responsible AI Development

With the increasing capabilities of LLMs, there is a heightened focus on the ethical implications of their deployment. Issues such as bias, fairness, transparency, and accountability are at the forefront of AI research and policy-making. Future trends are likely to see the development of more robust frameworks for ethical AI, including improved methods for detecting and mitigating bias in training data and algorithms.

Regulatory bodies and international organizations are expected to play a crucial role in establishing guidelines and standards for the responsible use of LLMs. This includes ensuring data privacy, preventing the misuse of AI technologies, and promoting transparency in AI decision-making processes. The establishment of interdisciplinary research groups, involving ethicists, technologists, and policymakers, will be essential in shaping the future landscape of AI governance.

Human-AI Collaboration

Rather than viewing LLMs as replacements for human workers, the future of AI is increasingly seen as a partnership between humans and machines. This trend towards human-AI collaboration is expected to enhance productivity, creativity, and problem-solving capabilities across various domains. LLMs can assist professionals by automating routine tasks, generating insights from vast datasets, and providing decision support, thereby augmenting human capabilities rather than replacing them.

In creative industries, LLMs are already being used to generate content, assist in writing, design, and even music composition. Future developments may see AI systems that work alongside artists, writers, and designers, providing new tools and perspectives that enhance the creative process. This symbiotic relationship could lead to unprecedented innovations and cultural outputs.

Expansion into New Domains

The scope of LLM applications is expected to expand into new and diverse domains. Beyond traditional areas like customer service, content generation, and language translation, LLMs are poised to make significant inroads into fields such as science, engineering, and the arts. For example, AI-driven research assistants could assist scientists in formulating hypotheses, analyzing data, and even designing experiments. In engineering, LLMs could be used to optimize designs and predict the behavior of complex systems. Moreover, the integration of LLMs with robotics and automation technologies could lead to the development of intelligent robotic systems capable of performing complex tasks in dynamic environments. This could have profound implications for industries such as manufacturing, logistics, and healthcare, where automation and precision are critical.

Improving Computational Efficiency

As LLMs grow in size and complexity, there is an increasing need to address the computational challenges associated with training and deploying these models. Future advancements are likely to focus on improving the efficiency of AI algorithms, reducing the computational resources required, and developing more scalable infrastructure. Techniques such as model pruning, quantization, and knowledge distillation are expected to play a crucial role in making LLMs more efficient without sacrificing performance.

Additionally, the development of specialized hardware, such as AI accelerators and neuromorphic chips, will continue to advance, enabling faster and more energy-efficient processing of large models. These innovations will be critical in making LLMs accessible and practical for a wider range of applications, from edge computing devices to cloud-based services.

Advancements in Language Understanding and Generation

The future of LLMs will likely see significant advancements in natural language understanding and generation. Models will become better at grasping nuances, idioms, and context, enabling more coherent and contextually relevant interactions. This will enhance the ability of LLMs to perform complex tasks such as conversational agents, real-time translation, and content generation with a deeper understanding of context and user intent.

Moreover, research into multi-lingual and cross-lingual models will continue to evolve, breaking down language barriers and fostering greater global communication. This could democratize access to information and services, bridging gaps between different cultures and languages.

Integration with Other Technologies

The convergence of LLMs with other emerging technologies, such as blockchain, Internet of Things (IoT), and quantum computing, is poised to unlock new possibilities. For instance, integrating LLMs with blockchain technology could enhance data security, privacy, and transparency in AI applications. In the IoT space, LLMs could enable smarter and more intuitive devices that can understand and respond to human commands and environmental cues more effectively.

Quantum computing, with its potential to handle vast amounts of data and perform complex calculations at unprecedented speeds, could revolutionize the training and inference processes of LLMs. This could lead to the development of models that are not only more powerful but also more efficient, overcoming some of the current limitations in AI research and application.

Societal and Economic Impacts

The widespread adoption of LLMs is expected to have profound societal and economic impacts. As AI technologies become more integrated into everyday life, issues such as job displacement, digital divide, and ethical considerations will become increasingly important. The future will likely see the development of new policies and frameworks to address these challenges, ensuring that the benefits of LLMs are distributed equitably across society.

Education and workforce development will play a crucial role in preparing individuals for the AI-driven economy. This includes fostering skills in AI literacy, critical thinking, and creativity, enabling people to thrive in an increasingly automated world. Additionally, public awareness and engagement with AI technologies will be essential in building trust and understanding, ensuring that the development and deployment of LLMs align with societal values and goals.

The journey of Large Language Models from their inception to their current state has been nothing short of transformative. As we look towards the future, the trends and predictions surrounding LLMs indicate a trajectory of continuous innovation and profound impact. From advancements in model architecture and multimodal integration to ethical considerations and societal impacts, LLMs are set to shape the next century in ways that are both exciting and challenging. Embracing these changes with a focus on responsible development and inclusive growth will be crucial in realizing the full potential of LLMs for the benefit of humanity.

About the Author

 Maria Johnsen, originating from Trondheim, Norway, boasts a diverse array of expertise encompassing AI computer engineering, film and TV investment, writing, directing, producing, poetry, and digital marketing. Growing up in a multilingual environment laid the foundation for Maria's linguistic prowess. Her academic journey traversed various disciplines, including Information Technology, Informatics, Beauty Arts and Culture, Computer Engineering, and Film Production.

Maria's exceptional contributions have earned her prestigious accolades such as the International Star Award for quality leadership, innovation, and excellence in 2019. Her impactful films, available on platforms like Amazon Prime, have captivated audiences in 175 countries. Complementing her filmmaking success, Maria has authored 64 books in English, German, French, Spanish, Japanese, and Dutch, including educational materials for postgraduate studies, showcasing her global influence as a published author.

Her literary repertoire extends to non-fiction works utilized in post-graduate programs at esteemed universities across North America and Europe. Titles such as "Search Engine Revolution," "The Business of Filmmaking: Building a Business and Networking Strategies in the Movie Industry," "AI in Digital Marketing," "The Future of Artificial Intelligence in Digital Marketing: The Next Big Technological Break," "Blockchain in Digital Marketing: A New Paradigm of Trust," "Multilingual Digital Marketing: Managing for

Excellence in Online Marketing," and "Sales in The Age Of Intelligent Web" underscore her expertise in digital marketing and emerging technologies.

Maria's educational journey transcended borders, with stints at institutions like Sorbonne University in Paris, Kharkov University in Ukraine, and engagements in Changchun, China, where she mastered Korean and Chinese. She has shared her knowledge by instructing English, French, and Russian to undergraduate and postgraduate students, notably achieving a 70% success rate with her students earning scholarships for further studies in the US and Canada.

As an entrepreneur, Maria founded Golden Way Media, a company dedicated to promoting businesses globally. Based in London, UK, she manages Golden Way Media Films and Golden Way Media, a digital marketing firm in Norway. Recognized as a top digital marketing influencer worldwide and among the top 100 global influencers in artificial intelligence (A.I.) and Fintech by Onalytica in 2016, Maria continues to excel across diverse domains, penning commercially viable screenplays and leaving an indelible mark on the cinematic landscape.

Bibliography

Aggarwal, Charu C. *Neural Networks and Deep Learning: A Textbook*. Cham: Springer, 2018.

Bird, Steven, Ewan Klein, and Edward Loper. *Natural Language Processing with Python*. Sebastopol, CA: O'Reilly Media, 2009.

Bishop, Christopher M. *Pattern Recognition and Machine Learning*. New York: Springer, 2006.

Devlin, Jacob, Ming-Wei Chang, Kenton Lee, and Kristina Toutanova. "BERT: Pre-training of Deep Bidirectional Transformers for Language Understanding."

arXiv:1810.04805 (2018).

Géron, Aurélien. *Hands-On Machine Learning with Scikit-Learn, Keras, and TensorFlow: Concepts, Tools, and Techniques to Build Intelligent Systems*. 2nd ed. Sebastopol, CA: O'Reilly Media, 2019.

Goodfellow, Ian, Yoshua Bengio, and Aaron Courville. *Deep Learning*. Cambridge, MA: MIT Press, 2016.

Hastie, Trevor, Robert Tibshirani, and Jerome Friedman. *The Elements of Statistical Learning: Data Mining, Inference, and Prediction*. 2nd ed. New York: Springer, 2009.

Johnsen, Maria. *The Future of Artificial Intelligence in Digital Marketing: The Next Big Technological Break*. 2017.

Jurafsky, Daniel, and James H. Martin. *Speech and Language Processing*. 3rd ed. Upper Saddle River, NJ: Prentice Hall, 2020.

Jurafsky, Daniel, and James H. Martin. *Speech and Language Processing: An Introduction to Natural Language Processing, Computational Linguistics, and Speech Recognition*. Upper Saddle River, NJ: Prentice Hall, 2021.

Russell, Stuart, and Peter Norvig. *Artificial Intelligence: A Modern Approach*. Upper Saddle River, NJ: Prentice Hall, 2021.

Vaswani, Ashish, Noam Shazeer, Niki Parmar, Jakob Uszkoreit, Llion Jones, Aidan N. Gomez, Lukasz Kaiser, and Illia Polosukhin. "Attention is All You Need." *arXiv:1706.03762* (2017).